Talking Faith

An Eight-Part Study on Growing & Sharing Your Faith

D1304647

Talking Faith

An Eight-Part Study on Growing & Sharing Your Faith

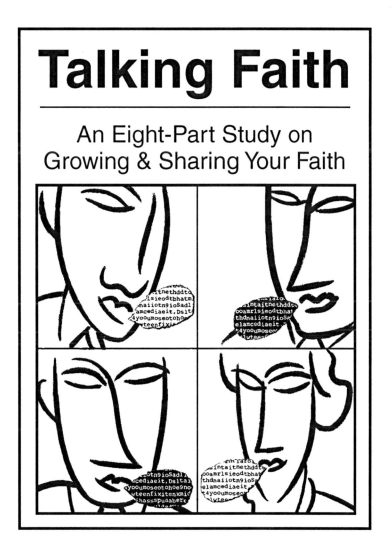

Heather Kirk-Davidoff

Nancy Wood-Lyczak

CHALICE
PRESS

ST. LOUIS, MISSOURI

With the generous support of the Curriculum Incubators Project, Christian Board of Publication, St. Louis, Missouri

Cover art: © Getty Images
Cover and interior design: Elizabeth Wright

Visit Chalice Press on the World Wide Web at
www.chalicepress.com

10 9 8 7 6 5 4 3 2   09 10 11 12 13 14

Library of Congress Cataloging-in-Publication Data

Kirk-Davidoff, Heather.
  Talking faith : an eight-part study on growing & sharing your faith / Heather Kirk-Davidoff, Nancy Wood-Lyczak.
    p. cm.
  ISBN 978-0-827236-54-7 (alk. paper)
  1. Evangelistic work. I. Wood-Lyczak, Nancy. II. Title.
  BV3795.K57 2004
  269'.2'0715—dc22
                                                              2004008678

Printed in the United States of America

Contents

About This Series

What This Series Is

The Components of the Series

Sessions Outline

Inviting People to Participate

Materials List for All Eight Sessions

What This Series Is

What this series is. And what it is not.

This is a series about evangelism. And then again, it isn't.

In the context in which we have served as ministers, evangelism is a dirty word. If you were to offer a course on evangelism in most of our churches, no one would come. The word signifies everything we don't want to be: dogmatic, doctrinal, disrespectful of other faiths, and convinced of our own superiority. A lot of horrible things have been done in the name of sharing the good news, and a lot of faithful Christian leaders would rather stay away from the activity altogether rather than deal with all the problems the activity presents.

But our churches are dying. Total membership in "mainline" denominations has been in decline for more than fifty years, and many of our congregations are just hanging on, living off of endowments and the memory of glory days gone by.

These undeniable facts have led many churches to look for programs that promise renewal. Time and again, however, traditional church growth tactics fall flat in congregations that have not nurtured a vital faith in their membership. Increasingly, church leaders are realizing that faith revitalization is critical to church revitalization.

And so, we're trying to find ways to grow spiritually. In recent years, interest in small groups, retreats, and other programs have ballooned. Our denominations offer weekends for women, for men, for singles, and for seniors, all promising to deepen the participants' relationship with God.

It's not enough to grow your faith. You need to share it.

It's not enough. As long as we merely emphasize spiritual growth, we reinforce the inward, self-focused orientation of our congregations, which is a central dynamic in their decline. What's more, the kind of faith we tend to foster is one that is more about ourselves than it is about the world. When we leave the group or finish the retreat, we find that our "spirituality" doesn't have legs to walk in the world.

Evangelism and spiritual growth are not competing activities. They are two sides of the same coin. In order to develop a faith that lives and grows right alongside our daily lives, we need to find a way to use it and act on it outside our churches. In order to do that, we need to find a way to express what we hold to be true in the words we use every day. We need to talk about it and not just with each other. We need to share our faith with the world.

Conversations about faith are not just about convincing other people that we are right and they are wrong—that's a speech, a tirade, an attack. A conversation is about exploration, engagement, and building relationship. When we have a conversation about faith, we discover what we really believe. We find out that some of what we thought we believed rings hollow when we say it out loud. We find out that some things we thought don't matter are of great interest to others. We find out that people often are yearning for conversation about things that really matter. We find out that we actually do have a faith to share.

When we have conversations about faith, we find out that spirituality really isn't just for ourselves. It's a gift we have to offer the world.

But I don't know enough!

We live in a day and age of experts. When we want advice about our health, our taxes, our time management, our children, we seek the advice of experts, those who have the degrees to show how much more they know than we do. When it comes to faith, we are keenly aware of our status as amateurs. We haven't read the whole Bible. We haven't studied much theology or church history. We couldn't distinguish the theologian Tillich from Troeltsch if our lives depended on it.

Thus, when urged to share their faith, many in our congregation respond, "But I don't know enough!" So, we offer classes, read books, bring in speakers, and show a twelve-week video series. People come, they take notes, and they seem interested. But at the end of the program, we find that all we've done is reinforce people's sense that they need more information before they can say anything about their faith. By bringing in the experts, we've only reinforced their identity as amateurs. We've only given them one more reason to keep their faith to themselves.

We don't need to learn more. We need to engage more.

This series will not help you to teach people what to believe. As the leader, you will not be called on to give out information. You will not be asked to answer questions. You will not be the expert, and as a result, this series will help all involved, even the leader, to grow and share their faith.

This is not to say that everyone involved will have an adequate understanding of the Bible, or even the basic tenets of the Christian faith. Those gaps exist, and in order to become mature Christians, many in our group will need to learn more about scripture, history, and tradition. But by encouraging them to begin sharing their faith, however tentative it may be, here and now, they will be motivated to learn more, not as a way to disengage, but as a way to engage more fully.

Plus, when we help people to share their faith starting now, even before they know everything, we're doing exactly what Jesus did. Even before they knew the end of the story, the disciples were on the road, sharing the gospel with whoever would listen. To be a disciple is to listen, learn, talk, and travel, all at the same time.

Living as a Christian takes practice.

This series is not just about what Christians believe. It is also about what they do. During each session, we will sing, pray, and share our faith with one another. These activities are not just devices for teaching. They are practices that form us as people of faith.

The range of Christian practices is wide and worthy of much exploration. They include such activities as hospitality, acts of compassion, and the care of the land. Within the context of this series, we will focus on three practices in particular that are key to developing faith: singing, praying, and faith sharing. It is important that you not skip over these parts of the course and just focus on discussion. By engaging with these practices, during the session and throughout the week, we'll move from thinking and talking about faith to living a life shaped and formed by faith.

Show, don't tell.

An additional and crucial component to fostering a vital faith within persons is mentoring by people who already have a deep, rich, and vital faith life. While there is no explicit provision for mentoring during the session, it is quite possible for it to happen. In fact, the success of the session is in part contingent on participants being mentored by you, the leader, and by other participants whom they come to trust and admire.

Leader as mentor

This series is not primarily about the dissemination of correct information about faith, and so it is a mistake to see the leader as an instructor and the participants as students. However, if the group is to function well, the leader will do more than simply guide a series of exercises. If you, as a leader, also participate in the exercises, you will find many opportunities to witness to your own faith. Do so gently—be careful about claiming the prerogative of the "last word" and be sure to share places where you have doubts or confusion, or where your mind has changed over time.

Participants as mentors

In addition to being mentored by the leader, the group members will also begin to mentor one another if they successfully build a strong level of trust and confidence in one another. This is not simply to say that those with a more seasoned faith will find opportunity to witness to the seekers in the group. Because the exercises do not rely on any prior knowledge, they tend to create a level playing field within the group. As a result, those who would claim to know the least about their faith may end up mentoring others in their openness to insight, their genuine curiosity, and their heartfelt desire to know God better.

Who is *Talking Faith* for?

Talking Faith is for anyone interested in exploring further what it means to have a vital Christian faith. There are no other prerequisites. So, once you have decided to offer *Talking Faith* in your congregation, think carefully about how you will publicize it and whom you will recruit. Considering offering a personal invitation to:

> *Core leaders:* Much of the time, the people who do all of the work of our churches have little opportunity to talk about their faith—all of their conversations within the church are about agendas and meetings and problems. Our core leaders are also among those who hold the most fear of not being "expert" enough. You may assume they are the most confident in their faith, but they may need *Talking Faith* the most.

> *Potential leaders:* You may also want to seek out members of your congregation who haven't stepped up to positions of leadership, but who you feel have the potential to do so. The certificate of completion of this series may be exactly what they need to feel qualified to take a new role in the congregation.

> *People on the edges:* This course is not only for convinced and confident Christians who need some practice sharing their faith. It is also appropriate for those who aren't sure if they are Christian, those who have just joined your church, those who are considering joining, and even those who are thinking about leaving. Be bold in your invitation to all of these people!

Adapt this curriculum to your church's needs.

Every group of people is different. And every church has different dynamics and different needs. You know your group best. Here are some suggestions of ways you might adapt this curriculum if you find that the standard format doesn't meet your needs.

If you need to teach fewer than eight sessions:

> This curriculum is highly adaptable and can be used for four or more sessions. If you aren't going to do all eight sessions, we suggest that at the opening session (session 1) you distribute the outline of the themes for all the subsequent sessions and have the participants choose the topics that are most relevant to them. If you plan to use this as a Lenten series, we suggest that you end with session 6. The communion service is a wonderful ending to a six-week series and readies your group for Holy Week.

If your group is shy:

> *Talking Faith* is highly participatory. You may find that you need to pace this to meet the individual needs of your group. If the sessions are moving too fast for the participants, move at a slower pace to fit the needs of your group. But don't give up! We know the rewards to

be big even when your group needs to take smaller steps to get there.

Remember: You have what you need.

At the end of *The Wizard of Oz,* Dorothy and each of her companions are presented with the gift each had been searching for. But as the Wizard points out, the Cowardly Lion had the courage he needed all along, he just didn't have a medal to prove it. And the Scarecrow had all the brains he needed; he just didn't have a diploma to show. At the end of the journey, they found out that they had what they needed all along.

If you offer this series in your congregation, you will attract people who feel like their faith needs help. People will sign up who feel like they don't know enough, don't believe enough, and haven't read enough. People will sign up who feel like everyone else is more of a Christian than they are, as will people who worry that someone will ask them a question and find out how little they know about the Bible, how unsure they are about Jesus, how tentative their own faith practice is.

At the end of the course, you will give each of these people a certificate. But you won't be recognizing how much they have accomplished and learned with the help of this series. You will be celebrating the faith that they have had all along and the growth in their confidence that they have something to share that the whole world is hungry for.

What a gift. May you receive the same for yourself.

The Components of the Series

The following is a list of the components that make up a group meeting and an explanation of what that section is about.

Group Meal

We know that people are busy and have a great many responsibilities in their lives. However, if you can possibly swing it, a group meal is a wonderful way to begin each meeting. A group meal provides people with time to transition from "the world out there" to "the world in here"—to talk about the details of their day and their week and get them out of the way before the session begins. A group meal also provides a way for people to trickle in without interrupting the group meeting itself. Most importantly, a group meal provides table fellowship and the opportunity to practice hospitality.

Tailor the group meal to your individual group. If they are a potluck crowd, do that. If people have more disposable income than they do time, pool your resources to order take-out for the group.

We know that you will find the added effort of a group meal worth it to the overall experience of the people in your group.

Opening Song

Singing is a great way to begin anything. Make sure you begin each meeting with a song. Write the song out in large letters on newsprint so that everyone can gather around the words to the song and sing out. Hang it up in a prominent place in your meeting space. Choose a hymn or praise chorus that ties in with the week's theme and is either reasonably well known or easy to learn. (Suggestions for songs are listed for each session.)

If you are having a meal together, use the opening song as your grace. Put the lyrics up right by your buffet line so that people can sing together and then start dishing out the food. If you are not eating together first, have everyone stand up and sing out as the first activity of the evening.

Schedule Review

People like to know what to expect. Remember Mr. Rogers' song, "I like to be told"? You will find an outline of each session at the beginning of each chapter. Take time to write out the schedule, and spend a few minutes going over it with the group. People can ask questions and it will help them feel that they are working together on the same project.

Large Talk

During "Large Talk" (as distinct from "small talk") the participants have the opportunity to answer a question that requires them to share something about themselves and their faith with another person. This allows the participants to get to know one another and provides a forum for them to practice telling other people things that are important to them. It also challenges the group members to cultivate a practice of listening. During this part of the session, members of the group are encouraged not to respond verbally to one another's comments but rather to simply listen fully to their partners in faith.

As the leader, you should make sure that everyone changes Large Talk partners each week so that each person has a chance to talk one-on-one with everyone in the group. Be clear how much time people have to talk and ring a soft bell at the end of the Large Talk to let people know that they need to conclude the conversation and come back to the large group.

When we first began teaching this course, one participant suggested that, at the close of each session, we let the group know what the Large Talk question would be for the next meeting time. A quiet, thoughtful person, she found it helpful to have some time to think about the Large Talk question ahead of time. You may want to do this with your group as well.

Theme Talk

We have chosen eight of the big questions of faith to examine in this series. During the Theme Talk, the participants will be given an opportunity to go in-depth on a particular topic, wrestle with the challenges of the question, hear what others have to say on the topic, and articulate what they believe. We use Bible study, interactive activities, and discussion to address the theme.

In all sessions, Jesus Christ and the Bible are central to the discussion. We examine Jesus' life, his ministry, his witness, his death, and his resurrection in light of the topic. It is our hope that this will help people see Jesus as the foundation on which all conversation about Christian faith builds.

Real World

The Real World part of the meeting offers people the chance to articulate what they believe about the week's theme. For each Real World segment, we have prepared questions to ask your group. These questions come directly out of conversations that we have had with real people. You can feel free to add questions of your own that you have had people ask you.

Make Real World as much like a game as possible. This will help people relax and speak from the heart without worrying about getting the "right" answer. Put the questions in a hat and have people pick (as in a charades game).

Different groups are going to have different levels of comfort with Real World questions. Some will be ready to dive right in to role plays, where one person asks the Real World question and another responds so that they begin a dialogue about faith. Others will need to work up to this level of faith dialogue. We give suggestions in the sessions about what kind of Real World activity to do for the week, but you will know your group best and know how to pace the discussion.

For Real World, everyone should begin with the assumption that the questioner is asking the questions in good faith. There is no attempt to "get" the person answering the question. Rather, the questioner is a seeker who has really been wondering about questions of faith and is excited to find a real, live Christian who wants to talk about faith questions.

Here is a list of the possible levels of faith sharing for Real World questions:

1. Have people take turns reading the questions and have everyone comment on them. Make sure that the quiet people get to talk.
2. Pretend the group members are a "Dear Faith" panel. Set up chairs in a line so that the room has a "panel feel" to it. The leader is the facilitator of the panel. Have the leader read questions and the members respond. This is not much different from level 1 above, but it feels a little more "official."
3. Have people role-play the questions. Ask for two volunteers—one to be the person with the question and one to be the churchgoer who answers. The question is a means for dialogue. Have the two role-playing persons talk back and forth about the topic. Stress that they make this as "real" as possible. The participants may know when it is time to end the scenario and they will stop. Sometimes you will need to jump in and end it. In all cases, thank the participants heartily for their risk taking. Clapping and positive comments from those watching are always welcome!
4. Fishbowl. This is an extension of level 3. In the Fishbowl, two people begin to role-play the question. When someone from the audience wishes, he or she can call out "freeze" and take the place of someone in the role play. Once the newcomer is seated, the conversation continues with this new voice and new perspective.

Prayer Practice

At the end of the first meeting, pair people with prayer partners. You can do this by playing a game to get into a mixed-up order or by counting off by twos. Try to mix people so that they are not with their spouse or their favorite friend in the group.

Explain that the prayer partners are to support each other throughout the series. Prayer partners are asked to be in contact during the week (in person, via phone calls, or at church on Sunday morning) to talk about the prayer practice for the week and what they are learning. Some people choose to make a standing date for a phone call. Others go with what works for the week ahead. In all cases, prayer partners should agree to pray for their partners each time they pray.

If you find any resistance to the prayer partners, ask the group to trust you on this one. We can tell you that prayer partners have been extremely meaningful for those who have participated in this series before. When people are praying with and for one another, the trust level and commitment to the group changes dramatically.

It is also possible to use these prayer exercises individually (participants pray at home but do not talk during the week with a member of the group about that experience) and debrief as a group. If you go this route, make sure to allot ten minutes at the beginning of each session for the group members to talk about how the prayer practice went.

Closing Prayer

We have included ideas for your closing prayer time each week. The way your group prays ties into the week's theme and can often act as a model for the prayer practice. We encourage you to try out these different ways of praying as a group as it will help the participants expand their understanding of group prayer.

Memory Gift

Author and church consultant Tom Bandy and others have noted that we are moving from a literate culture to a visual culture. In a post-"word" culture, objects become more meaningful and can carry special significance for us. Plus, most people love a little gift.

We have included instructions for a Memory Gift for each session. This object is to act as a reminder for what the group has talked about at its meeting and to help the participants stay connected to the group over the week that follows. Each object can be made in an hour or purchased for less than one dollar.

We encourage you to give a Memory Gift at the close of each meeting. People really appreciate it and it helps to build momentum and commitment to the group.

Prayer Journals

The Memory Gift in session 1 is a prayer journal. These don't need to be anything fancy, just notebooks from the stationery or office supply store. (We do recommend that they be notebooks that are 7 3/4" x 5" because we have formatted the prayer practice sheets for each week to fit that size notebook.) Each week, the participants will be given a prayer activity for the week, found at the end of each session chapter in the manual.

We suggest that you photocopy and cut out the prayer practice for each week and have one for each participant. After you have explained what the prayer practice activity is for the week, have the participants glue the sheet into their journal. Now they are set to go. They are encouraged to write their feelings, thoughts, and responses to the week's prayer practice.

You can also tailor the prayer journals to fit the needs of your group. One test group chose to record their thoughts and insights in their prayer journals, but instead of pasting the prayer practice sheet into their journals, they printed them out in wallet size format and carried them around with them in their wallets and purses all week. Whenever and wherever they were, they could refer to the prayer practice and pray right then and there. That approach worked for them. We encourage you to model the prayer practice and prayer journals in the way that will best suit your group and allow them to integrate prayer into their lives.

No matter your format, emphasize that the prayer journal is only for the owner of the notebook. No one else will read it. No one will collect it or grade it. Ask them to bring the journals to each session.

Sessions Outline

1. **What do I need to know?**

   When it comes to faith, what do you wonder about? What do you feel sure about? How do you balance your need to know with your need to wonder?

2. **How do we know anything about God?**

   Where do we get information about who God is? How can we understand the claims about God that other people make?

3. **What does God do?**

   How do we understand God's power? How does that relate to our understanding of human power? Can we talk about this with other people?

4. **Why do bad things happen?**

   How can we make sense of bad things that happen in our life and in our world? How does God respond to suffering? How should we?

5. **Who's to say what is right and wrong?**

   How does our faith affect the way we live our lives? How do our faith and our culture interact? When they conflict, what do we do?

6. **Who's invited?**

   Who is faith for? Is this about us or about the world? Is everyone welcome? What difference does it make?

7. **What about all the other religions?**

   Does it make sense to be a particular religion? How should we respond to people of other religions? Is there only one way or many ways to God?

8. **What can I hope for?**

   Is there such a thing as heaven? Where? What difference does it make?

Inviting People to Participate

(The following article can be reprinted for use in your church newsletter or bulletin.)

Would you like to talk with people in our congregation about more than the next committee meeting? Would you like to spend some time considering big questions with great people in fun ways? Would you like to deepen your faith and grow in your ability to share it? Join us for *Talking Faith,* an eight-week course that promises to energize us and get us talking with one another about things that really matter.

Each session will last $2^1/_2$ hours and will include a meal, some fun activities, and great conversation. Together, we will address such topics as "How Do We Know Anything about God?" "What Does God Do?" and "Who's to Say What Is Right and Wrong?"

Here is what people who have participated in *Talking Faith* have said about the series.

"I think my relationship with Jesus developed a lot as a result of the class."

"This class was God's way of answering my prayer because I had been praying for something that would give me the opportunity to share my faith with others. I believe this class allowed me to do that."

"I thought this class was going to be a stuffy lecture type—I was pleasantly surprised!"

Materials List for All Eight Sessions

Session Supplies

- Bell
- Black writing markers
- Colored pencils or crayons
- Colored sticky dots
- Colored sticky notes
- Glue sticks
- Heavy stock paper in green, red, and yellow (to be used for sessions 6 and 7)
- White paper
- Laminating sheets (no heat)
- Large black markers for writing on newsprint
- Masking tape
- Newsprint
- Easel
- Name tags
- Bibles, one for each member of the group
- Basket
- Large candle and matches
- CD or audiocassette player and meditative music
- Stuffed animal or toy lamb
- Gauze or bandage
- Modeling clay
- Vine or a leafy plant
- Paper star
- Shepherd, Mary, Joseph, Jesus, and angel from crèche set
- Toy hen or a picture of a hen
- Loaf of bread
- Bowl of water and towel
- Cross
- Communion set, bread, and juice
- Camera
- Dark glasses, trench coat, or other disguise outfit
- Paper towels

Additional Memory Gift Supplies

- Prayer Practice notebooks for the participants (We suggest notebooks that are 7³/₄" x 5" because the prayer practice sheets are formatted for that size)
- Invitation cards
- Ivy sprigs—either fresh or silk or plastic
- Lapel pins—with a Christian symbol, can be ordered from www.automonline.com
- Small votive candles for each person in your group
- Magnetic tape or refrigerator photo magnets
- Self-laminating sheets for bookmarks and laminated prayer cards

"What Do I Need to Know?"

Welcome—5 minutes

Song—5 minutes

Meal—30 minutes

Large Talk—Pearly Gates questions—10 minutes

Theme Talk—30 minutes

> What do you *really* need to know?—5 minutes
>
> Certainty and mystery in daily life—15 minutes
>
> Certainty and mystery in the Bible—10 minutes

Real World—30 minutes

> Sticky note exercise—15 minutes
>
> Response—15 minutes

Prayer Practice—10 minutes

Closing Prayer—5 minutes

Memory Gift—Prayer journals

"What Do I Need to Know?"

OBJECTIVES

To orient the participants to the session format and expectations, to help the participants identify how their needs for certainty and for mystery impact their faith, and to consider how they might talk about faith issues with people who have a different orientation toward certainty and mystery than they do.

MATERIALS

- Newsprint flipchart
- Easel
- Masking tape
- Big black marker
- Name tags or table tents
- Lots of different colored self-stick note papers
- Permanent markers, one for each participant
- Small notebooks or journals (optional: gift wrapped)
- Glue or tape

PREPARATION

- Write on newsprint the lyrics to an opening song. Hang the printed lyrics up in a prominent place.
- Set up the newsprint and easel, and chairs if you need to.
- Prepare the prayer journals: Purchase a notebook for each participant, having a few extras just in case. (We suggest notebooks that are 7³/₄" x 5" because the Prayer Practice sheets are formatted for that size.) Glue or tape the Prayer Practice information in each journal. See page 18 for Prayer Practice.
- The participants will use the prayer journals daily throughout the course to note any comments or insights about their daily prayer time. While the notebooks need not be fancy, consider if there is some way to make them feel special to the participants. Possibilities include wrapping them up as gifts each with a participant's name on it, tying them with ribbon, or adding stickers or some other symbol to the front cover. Keep it simple, but even a small gesture in this respect will increase the chance that the participants will use the journal and not lose it!

Session Outline

Welcome

As the participants enter the room, encourage each one to fill out a name tag. If you plan to spend most of the session sitting around a table, you might decide instead to make table tents (Fold a piece of card stock into thirds along the length of the paper). It's a good idea to have name tags or "tents" even if you think everyone knows one another.

Song

We highly recommend that you begin your session with a song. Especially for this opening session, the song should be something that everyone knows and that is easy to sing. Don't assume everyone knows all the words, however! If you are sharing a meal, use this song as your blessing. If people are trickling in as you eat, sing the song before and after the meal! Songs you might use include "Amazing Grace," "Dona Nobis Pacem," "The Doxology," "Amen, Amen," "Come, All Ye People."

Meal

Large Talk

Divide the group into pairs or triads, and invite everyone to share their "Pearly Gates Questions," that is, questions they would love to ask God, if they could. Lead off the activity with a few examples of your own, and be sure to include some light ones such as:

> "Why did you make mosquitoes?"

> "Could I have a do-over?"

Give the participants five to seven minutes to talk—and give a warning two minutes before ending so that everyone in the groups has a chance to suggest at least one question.

Theme Talk

What do you really need to know?

As the group comes together, ask a few people to share any questions that were particularly memorable. Did any really make you laugh? Did anyone hear a question that she or he also would want to ask? You don't need a thorough reporting from each group—just a few highlights.

After hearing a few questions, ask the group members to reflect on which questions they felt like they really need answers to, and which ones were just fun to muse over. Depending on the group's comfort level at this point, someone may want to share his or her responses to this question. Otherwise, you can simply offer the observation that different questions have different levels of urgency.

Certainty and mystery in daily life

This observation leads nicely into an introduction to our variable needs for certainty and mystery. Note that in some areas of life we really do need certainty—traffic laws, for example. Can your group think of other places where they really are not comfortable with mystery? You might list these things on newsprint under the title "I want certainty."

In other areas of life, however, we really do not need certainty. In fact, we need something else, a kind of openness to inquiry that might be described as mystery. Things that are mysterious are intriguing. They draw us in with our inquiring and wondering, but resist simple solutions or answers. For example, we watch our children grow up and we wonder what they will be like when they are adults. Although sometimes our wondering about this even has a kind of urgency, we are not really in need of a clear and specific answer to our question.

Can your group think of other places where we need to wonder? You might list these things on newsprint under the title "I want mystery." This list might be a little harder to generate, so be prepared with some suggestions of your own: What about love? (Do you need to fully know and understand a person to fall in love with him or her? Or is appreciating the unfolding mystery part of the appeal?) What about the future? (Would you look into a crystal ball if you could, or do you appreciate watching life unfold in ways you wouldn't necessarily predict?) What about art? (Does it help to know what a picture is about, or would you rather figure it out on your own?)

After you have the two lists, you might have some fun throwing out areas that could go on either side, and see if different people in the group would place them differently. For example, where would people place personal finances? What about cooking?

Certainty and mystery in the Bible
Finally, ask

> What about faith? In your faith lives, where would you place yourselves? Certainty or mystery or somewhere in between?

You can just throw this question out, and see if anyone bites. If no one does, just move on to the next section.

Ask the group,

> Do you think the Bible is more concerned with certainty or with mystery?

Let the group discuss this, and perhaps brainstorm about which part of the Bible would fall into which category.

Then ask,

> Where do you think Jesus belongs?

While some members may respond to this question generally, press them for examples. You may also throw out your own. Are the parables more about certainty or mystery? What about Jesus' response to the rich young ruler? What about his healing ministry? What about his death on the cross? What about his resurrection?

We hope these questions will not only spark some good debate but also lead the group to note that Jesus appealed to both certainty and mystery at different times in his ministry and life.

Real World

Pass out sticky notes and permanent markers to the participants. (It's fun for the participants to have different color sticky notes—let them pick!) Flip the newsprint to a new page and create two columns with the headings, "I Wonder…" and "I Know for Sure…"

Invite the participants to complete both sentences on their sticky notes. They can finish each sentence any number of times; just suggest they use a different sticky note for each one. Allow people three to four minutes to write, and then invite them to stick their notes in the proper column.

When all the notes are up, ask for a volunteer to read all of the "I Wonder" sentences aloud. Pause without comment for a moment, and then ask the volunteer to read all the "I Know for Sure" sentences aloud. Often, these statements make quite an impact when they are all read aloud together. Allow a moment for them to sink in, and then give the group some strong affirmation about the power and importance of what they are able to proclaim. If you can genuinely do so, tell them that their affirmations can make a difference to our hurting world.

This is a great time to start affirming the participants' abilities to share their faith—even now, before they "know everything." Choose one of the following to do with your group:

- Pair the members up, and have them say aloud one of their "I Know for Sure" statements to their partners, looking them in the eye. Ask the partners to tell the speakers what it felt like to hear the statements.
- Ask, "Who in the world needs to hear these things? In whose life would a statement like this mean a great deal?" You might point to various statements and ask the group to brainstorm who might need to hear each one, or consider the statements as a whole.
- Ask members if they know someone who

they think needs to hear these statements. There might be a story some would want to share.

- Ask the group to consider together: How would the world be different if everyone could say they believed all these things? Who would you most wish could make these affirmations (a political leader? your child?)?

Let this part be very gentle and open-ended. Our goal at this time is simply to build a desire to share faith, not to present a challenge to do so. When there is about fifteen minutes left, draw the conversation to a close.

Prayer Practice

This week, we will spend some time establishing this practice. First, we will pair the participants as "prayer partners." It is best to do this randomly, and it will probably help the group to focus if they can stand up and move a little. You might suggest that they line up according to birthdays—month and day only! For a twist, suggest that the group line up in this manner without speaking, but using only hand signals. Then, pair people down the line. Be sure that spouses and partners are separated!

Hand out the small notebooks that will become prayer journals. Ask all the partners to sit down together and exchange contact information. Written on the first page will be the day's date and the prayer homework for the coming week:

> Write a question addressed to God. Sit quietly with the question for at least ten minutes. Write down any thoughts or observations afterward, including comments about the experience of prayer.

Take some time to talk honestly with the participants about how it can be hard to find even ten minutes of quiet time. Suggest some strategies, including setting the alarm fifteen minutes earlier in the morning, sitting in the car

for ten minutes after arriving at work or returning home, spending an extra ten minutes in the shower or bathtub.

Give the prayer partners a few minutes to talk to each other about when they are most likely to find the time to pray, and then ask them to be accountable to each other for this daily practice. Ask them to establish a time when they will contact each other during the week to talk, even briefly, about their experience of the Prayer Practice. Importantly, request that each prayer partner pray for his or her partner daily.

Ask the participants to open their notebooks and find this week's Prayer Practice. Take time to answer any questions that might arise.

Closing Prayer

Invite the group to stand and join hands, and take a moment of silence to gather thoughts. Then, lead the group in prayer. You may simply wish to pray for the whole group this time, or you might want to lead off with a short prayer, and then squeeze the hand of the person next to you, indicating that they might add a prayer of their own. If they would like to pass, they simply squeeze the hand of the next person in the circle, and so on. When the hand squeeze comes back to you, conclude the prayer simply.

If anyone has brought up points of pain or friends in trouble, be sure to pray for those things.

Memory Gift

This week we hand out the prayer journals. See the "preparation" section of the session for information. Encourage the group members to bring their journals to every session.

Write down any thoughts or observations afterward, including comments about the experience of prayer.

Prayer Practice

Session 1 Prayer Practice

- Write a question addressed to God.
- Sit quietly with the question for at least ten minutes.
- Write down any thoughts or observations afterward, including comments about the experience of prayer.

Session 1 Prayer Practice

- Write a question addressed to God.
- Sit quietly with the question for at least ten minutes.
- Write down any thoughts or observations afterward, including comments about the experience of prayer.

Session 1 Prayer Practice

- Write a question addressed to God.
- Sit quietly with the question for at least ten minutes.
- Write down any thoughts or observations afterward, including comments about the experience of prayer.

"How Do We Know Anything about God?"

Song—5 minutes

Meal—30 minutes

Large Talk—Share a time you learned something—10 minutes

Theme Talk—40 minutes

> How did you learn that?—10 minutes
>
> What do folks in churches have to say?—10 minutes
>
> What about Jesus?—10 minutes
>
> What about you?—5 minutes
>
> What about others?—5 minutes

Real World—20 minutes

Prayer Practice—10 minutes

Closing Prayer—10 minutes

Memory Gift—Bookmarks

"How Do We Know Anything about God?"

OBJECTIVES

For the participants to locate the sources of religious authority in their lives and to consider what it means to dialogue about faith with people who understand religious authority differently than they do.

MATERIALS

- Newsprint sheet with the two columns "I wonder" and "I know for sure..." from session 1
- Newsprint flipchart
- Easel
- Masking tape
- Bell
- White paper
- Colored pencils
- Self-stick notes with crosses
- Bibles for everyone
- Memory Gift—see page 27 for an example
- Large candle and matches
- Prayer Practice sheets
- Glue sticks
- Basket or cup
- Laminating sheets

PREPARATION

- Write song lyrics on newsprint.
- Make bookmarks as a closing gift. As our Prayer Practice this week is *lectio divina,* we suggest that you make bookmarks with the essential questions of *lectio divina* written on them. Sample bookmarks and questions are included at the end of this session on page 27. You can use that one or create your own. It is a good idea to laminate the bookmark so that it will hold up. You can purchase self-laminating sheets at the local office store, and use them to laminate your bookmarks.
- Put crosses on sticky notes.
- Set up the newsprint and easel, and chairs if you need to.
- Have a Bible for everyone. Mark each Bible at Acts 2:43–47 with a gift bookmark.
- Prepare the questions for the Real World role plays. Copy the Real World questions found on pages 25–26, and cut the questions apart. Fold them and put them in a basket or cup.

Session Outline

Song

Suggestions for this week's song include "Over My Head" ("I Hear Music in the Air") and "Jesus Loves Me!"

Meal

Large Talk

Divide the group into pairs (make sure that people are not talking to the same folks they did last week). Have each person in the pair answer the following question:

> Share a time you learned something in your life. For example: A time you learned a moral lesson, how to do an activity, or how to make a craft. How did you learn it?

Give participants eight to ten minutes for Large Talk. Ring the bell softly to end the time.

Theme Talk

How did you learn that?

Spend a little time having people talk about what they have learned and how they learned it. Notice commonalties—learning from books, learning from other people, being self-taught.

Bring up the idea of authority. When we learn something a certain way, we give authority to that method of learning. For example, some people give a lot of authority to teachers or "educated people" and will want to learn a new thing from an expert. Others place authority in themselves and will be comfortable teaching themselves something. Ask the question,

> To what do you give authority?

Hang up the newsprint from the first session that says, "I know for sure…" Read off the answers that members gave to that statement. Note that they came up with powerful statements about God and faith. Ask them,

> How did you learn that?

Write their answers on a new sheet of newsprint. Again, see if there are commonalties or common ways people learn things when it comes to their relationship with God.

What do folks in churches have to say?

On a new sheet of newsprint, draw John Wesley's Four Ways of Knowing. (See the diagram on page 24.)

Explain that scripture, reason, experience, and tradition are ways of knowing God. These are realms of authority for knowing God that the church has recognized since its beginnings. You may want to give examples of each of the four ways of knowing God. Try to think of examples from your own life. For example, someone's first experience of the resurrection might come through reading about it in scripture. Another person might reason out the existence of God.

Invite the participants to name aloud ways that they have come to know God through scripture, reason, experience, and tradition. Write those examples in each of the four sections on the newsprint.

These four ways of knowing God work together. Most of us may emphasize one particular way of knowing God over another, but we use all of them to enhance our understanding of who God is and how God makes God's self known to us.

Take as much time on this part of the session as you need. Make sure that each participant understands the four ways of knowing and has had a chance to talk about them. If they give examples of people they know or have come in contact with who have emphasized a particular way of knowing God, write that on the newsprint as well. We will spend some time on that when we talk about "What about others?"

Be sure that people clarify their ways of knowing God through scripture. Have people note in particular how and why they value scripture the way they do.

What about Jesus?

Now ask people where Jesus fits on the newsprint. Pass out the sticky notes with crosses to the participants and ask them to place the notes on the newsprint where they think the notes most represent Jesus' way of knowing God.

To get the conversation rolling, you may want to ask:

> Why did you put Jesus where you did on the graph?

> Can you give an example in Jesus' life when he demonstrates one of the four ways of knowing God?

Perhaps the group will come to see that, like us, Jesus used all four ways of knowing God at different times in his life. Here are a few examples of times Jesus used the four ways of knowing:

- Scripture—Jesus reads Isaiah in the temple and understands his work in light of the text.
- Experience—Jesus prays, Jesus is baptized.
- Reason—Jesus wants to engage with people about God. He asks questions to get people talking about religious law and then points out when there is a logical inconsistency to the law.
- Tradition—Jesus celebrates Passover.

What about you?

Pass out blank white paper and plenty of colored pencils. Invite the participants to draw a pie chart. Then have them divide the pie four ways, showing the ways of knowing God that best describe their understanding. For example, someone who puts a large importance on personal experience might make the "experience" slice of his pie very large. Someone who reads the Bible daily and uses it for guidance might give extra weight to her "scripture" slice of pie. Emphasize that the only requirement is that everyone has four slices in her or his pie. The size of the slices is up to each person—he or she can divide the pie any way that is most representative of the way he or she understands authority. Have folks label each section of their pies.

When they are done, ask them to share their pies with the group. Have them answer the following questions:

> Where do you place the most emphasis?

> Why did you make what was big, big? Why did you make what was small, small?

What about others?

After everyone has had a chance to explain his or her pie chart, broaden the conversation, and invite people to reflect on the following questions:

> Have you ever had a conversation with someone whose largest slice of pie is your smallest? What did it feel like? If you have never had such a conversation, what do you imagine it would be like?

> How does it feel to talk to people who value a different way of knowing God?

Real World

Tell the group that they have been chosen to be part of a "Dear Faith" column in the local paper. Today they are meeting to discuss the faith questions that have been submitted to the paper. It is their job to give faith advice to the people who have written in. Everyone is needed to weigh in on the questions submitted.

Have a volunteer pick a "Dear Faith" question (see pages 25 and 26) out of the basket or cup and read it aloud. Then have as many members of the group who wish answer the question. Make sure to draw out the quieter members of the group. See if your "panel" can come up with one answer for the column. If not, highlight some of the differences in belief in the group. Have the group answer at least three of the questions. For fun, find out if the group members have their own questions that they would like to submit to "Dear Faith." Have the group consider those too.

Prayer Practice

This week our Prayer Practice is *lectio divina*. Because this type of prayer will be new to many in the group, we suggest that you use this practice as the group's Closing Prayer.

Pass out the Prayer Practice sheets. Provide glue sticks so that the participants can immediately glue their Prayer Practice into their prayer journals. Tell the group your Prayer Practice today is going to follow the form of the ancient practice called *lectio divina*, which means "Sacred Reading." This is reading a scripture as a spiritual practice. Tell them, "You read the text slowly, letting the words sink into your consciousness, meditate on words or phrases from the scripture that speak to your life, and lift to God in prayer the ideas or concerns that come to your mind during this reflection."

Closing Prayer

Now, turn down the lights (if possible) while still leaving enough light for people to read.

Light the candle. Hand out Bibles that have Acts 2:43–47 marked with the gift bookmarks.

Explain that we will be praying this week in a way that may be new to some folks. We will use our session time to model this ancient way of praying. Ask for two volunteers to read the passage. Have volunteer 1 read it and then pause for a few minutes of silence. Now have volunteer 2 read it. After another minute of silence, ask the first *lectio divina* question, "What does the text say?" Ask people to speak from the heart about what they think the text says. After that conversation has concluded, take another moment of silence and move to the question, "What does the text say to me?" Finally, end with, "What does God wish me to hear?"

When it feels appropriate, say, "Amen" and wish people a safe journey home.

Memory Gift

The Memory Gift for this week is the Bible bookmark found on page 27.

Scripture

Experience

Tradition

Reason

Real World Questions

Cut these questions apart and place them in a bowl or basket.

Dear Faith:

My aunt does this thing that when she has a problem and she needs an answer, she goes to the Bible and opens it up at random. She reads what is on that page and she says that is how God speaks to her. Is that how you read the Bible? Is everything in it true?

Signed, Jumbled by Genesis

Dear Faith:

My mom has cancer and she is not very religious, but she was asking me some questions about the Bible. She thinks she might like to read it while she is having the chemo treatments. How do you read the Bible?

Signed, New to the New Testament

Dear Faith:

I just can't buy everything that the Bible says. I mean, I don't believe the world was created in six days. I am with Darwin on that one. How can you believe in science and still have a faith in God?

Signed, Enamored of Evolution

Real World Questions

Dear Faith:

I have a friend who says that she prays to Jesus and he talks back to her. Is that possible? How does she know that it is really Jesus? Who is to say it is true?

Signed, Not Sure I Have a Friend in Jesus

Dear Faith:

My reason and intellect says there is a God. If the world exists, someone has to have created it. But I think believing in the resurrection of Jesus defies reason. I don't know anyone who has ever been resurrected. And I don't see how you can prove it. How can I believe in something that I can't rationally make sense of?

Signed, Needing Reassurance about the Resurrection

Bookmark

Lectio Divina

What does the
text say?

———

What does the
text say to me?

———

What does God
wish me to hear?

———

Lectio Divina

What does the
text say?

———

What does the
text say to me?

———

What does God
wish me to hear?

———

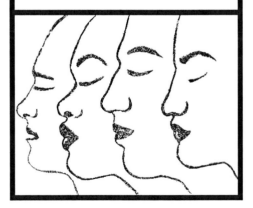

Session 2 Prayer Practice

- Find the time this week to use *lectio divina* to pray with Acts 2:43–47.

- How does your relationship to the passage change over time?

- How do you change by praying it daily?

Session 2 Prayer Practice

- Find the time this week to use *lectio divina* to pray with Acts 2:43–47.

- How does your relationship to the passage change over time?

- How do you change by praying it daily?

Session 2 Prayer Practice

- Find the time this week to use *lectio divina* to pray with Acts 2:43–47.

- How does your relationship to the passage change over time?

- How do you change by praying it daily?

(Permission is granted to photocopy this page for use with *Talking Faith*.)

"What Does God Do?"

Song—5 minutes

Meal—30 minutes

Large Talk—Pictures of God—10 minutes

Theme Talk—40 minutes

> Compare pictures—5 minutes
>
> What does the Bible say?—20 minutes
>
> Graphing divine and human power—15 minutes

Real World—20 minutes

Prayer Practice—5 minutes

Closing Prayer—10 minutes

Memory Gift—Sprigs of ivy

"What Does God Do?"

OBJECTIVES

For the participants to clarify and deepen their own understanding of how God acts in the world and to consider how they might talk with people who understand God's agency differently than they do.

MATERIALS

- Newsprint
- Masking tape
- Easel
- Big black marker
- White paper—recycled scrap paper is fine
- Sticky dots (Often these come in packs with four colors. You will need three colors for the exercise. We use red, blue, and yellow.)
- A bucket of crayons, colored pencils, or markers, whatever you can find.
- A CD or audiocassette player and some music, preferably without words (optional)
- Bibles for everyone—different translations or versions are fine
- Glue sticks or tape
- Ivy—either a living, potted plant from which you could make clippings (Swedish ivy works well for this purpose) or artificial ivy, available anywhere that sells silk flowers.
- Paper towels
- Basket for questions

PREPARATION

- Write the song lyrics on newsprint, and hang them in a prominent place in your meeting room.
- Set up the newsprint and easel, and chairs if you need to.
- Prepare the questions for the Real World role plays. Copy the questions from pages 35–36, and cut the questions apart. Fold them and put them in a basket or cup.
- Copy this week's Prayer Practice, page 37, and cut out one for each person in the group.
- Get this week's Memory Gift ready. If you are using artificial ivy, snip it into pieces about two inches long or so. If you are using a live vine, snip off pieces and wrap the cut ends in damp paper towels.

Session Outline

Song

Suggestions for this week's song include: "He's Got the Whole World in His Hand" and "Rise and Shine."

Meal

Large Talk

Pass out the white paper and the crayons, colored pencils, or markers. Make sure there are enough to go around and within easy reach. Invite the participants to draw something that expresses their understanding of God. How would they image God? Be careful about explaining this exercise too much—let the *participants* interpret the instructions as they like. Give everyone about five minutes to draw. You might find it helpful to play some music softly while people do this.

When most people are finished, group the participants in pairs or triads, and ask them to discuss with one another what their drawings say about God's power.

> What kind of power is expressed in their pictures?
>
> How does that power influence their lives?

This question may surprise some participants, and you might find it helpful to write it on a piece of newsprint. However, reveal the question only after the group has made their drawings!

Theme Talk

Compare pictures

After about five to seven minutes of conversation, bring the group back together. Ask for a few people to share their insights from the exercise. Not everyone needs to report back, but if the group is small enough, you may find it engaging to allow everyone to share. Chances are there will be some diversity within the group—people will have different understandings of God's power. Draw some of these differences out, being careful

not to evaluate them. Note that power can be modeled in all kinds of different ways. At the end of the session you will want to keep these pictures for use in next week's session.

What does the Bible say?

Noting the diversity of the group's insights will lead naturally to noting that there is also diversity in the ways in which God's power is represented in the Bible. Pass out Bibles to everyone, and ask them to open to the first chapter of the first book of the Bible.

Our goal will be to contrast God's power as it is described in the first and second creation stories in Genesis. We want to do so, however, without taking the time to read each story in its entirety—that will take too much time! So see if you can pull these stories out of your group, allowing them to refer to their Bibles as they answer your questions. Ask, "How does God create the world in the first story?" (You may get a variety of answers.) Then, ask the participants to act out how they imagine God in this first story. This may take some encouraging from you, but eventually you may be able to get people to wave their arms and point ("Shazam!") like a magician.

Then, turn to the second creation story in Genesis. People may be less familiar with this version, so they may need some directing to its beginning at Genesis 2:7. Have someone read the verses aloud, and then again ask the group to act out how they imagine God in the story. You may find that people use very different gestures—such as holding the clay man up to their mouths and gently blowing air in ("Puff!").

Ask the group to repeat these different gestures, or even label one side of the room "Shazam" and the other "Puff" and have a little fun feeling the difference between the two actions. Then ask, "Which action better describes the kind of power Jesus used?" Who votes for Shazam? Who votes for Puff?

Complicate the discussion by tossing out some stories about Jesus, and ask the group to pantomime the kind of power Jesus uses in each. Try these stories:

- Mark 9:2–8 (The transfiguration)
- John 8:1–11 (Jesus responds to the woman caught in adultery)
- John 9:1–7 (Jesus heals the blind man, touching his eyes with mud)
- Mark 1:21–28 (Jesus commands the unclean spirit to come out)

And to complicate things a little more:

- Matthew 14:22–33 (Jesus calms the storm, then gives Peter a hand)
- Luke 23:39–43 (Jesus won't take himself off the cross, but he invites the criminal next to him into Paradise)

Group members may have suggestions for other Bible passages that present a contrasting image of power. Don't get bogged down in this discussion—the point is simply to evoke the contrast. Have some fun with the "shazam" vs. "puff" contrast.

Now, introduce another wrinkle: human power. Note that the ways in which we understand God's power strongly affect our understanding of what humans are capable of, and vice versa.

Go to the newsprint and draw a graph like the one on page 34. Explain that some people understand humans as having all the power and God having none—those people would locate themselves far out on the X axis (human axis), with no value given to the Y axis (God's power) at all. Ask,

> Does anyone know anyone like that? An atheist, maybe? Or someone who believes that God exists but takes a completely "hands off" approach to the world?

Other people believe that God has all the power and humans have none—those people would locate themselves far out on the Y axis, with no value given to the X. (Again, you will want to keep this chart for future sessions).

Ask,

> Does anyone know someone like that, for example, a person who refuses to close the windows of her house during a hurricane because if God wants to take her, God will, and if God wants to spare her, God will?

Graphing divine and human power

The rest of us, of course, would locate ourselves somewhere in between these two extreme positions. Distribute to the participants sheets of dot stickers. Ask them to take the red one, and to stick it on the graph in the place where they would generally locate themselves. Allow a few minutes for this to happen (and put your own sticker on there!) and then stick one sticker at the bottom of the graph as the key—Write "IN GENERAL" next to it.

Next, ask the participants to recall a strong experience in their past—one of great joy, great pain, and so on. Note that they will not be asked to share what the experience was. Then ask them to locate on the graph with their blue dot how they understood the mix of God's power and human power in that experience. After people have finished, stick an extra blue dot at the bottom of your page as a key, and write "STRONG EXPERIENCE" next to it.

If the group still seems engaged in the activity, try for yellow dots. You might suggest that the group members graph their understanding of power in their "RELATIONSHIP WITH JESUS." Or, have them graph their understanding of divine and human power and their relationship to "HEALING." Or, take a suggestion from the group for some other category.

When all of the graphing is done, take a few minutes to step back and see if the group can notice any patterns among the dots.

- What conclusions can you draw?
- Where is there the greatest agreement among the group?
- Where is there the greatest disagreement?

- Do any group members want to share something about why they put a dot where they did?

Real World

By this time in the study, the group will probably be ready to really engage with some role plays, so be sure to time the preceding discussion so that you end with at least a half hour left of the session.

If the group still seems timid, you may want to have them be a "panel" again, one in which anyone can throw out a response to a question. But if you give them lots of affirmation about how comfortable they are becoming when talking about their faith, and if you explicitly acknowledge that you are asking them to take a risk, you will probably be able to get them to do role plays this week.

Here is how the exercise works: Show the group the basket with the questions. Explain that each question is one that has been asked by a seeker, and it relates to the question, "What does God do?" Explain that you need two volunteers, one to ask the question and one to take a stab at responding to it. Emphasize that the responder needs only to give it a try—there's no right answer! After the responder attempts an answer, the rest of the group will have a chance to contribute.

The success of this exercise rests, in large part, on the leader's ability to affirm each response. You may even encourage the group to do this by asking after each role play, "What worked well in this conversation?" Then you can ask, "What would you add?" Keep the pace moving and try to run through at least three questions.

Prayer Practice

Pass out this week's Prayer Practice and glue sticks or tape, and invite the group members to put the Prayer Practice into their prayer journals. When people have more or less done this, invite one person in the group to read the Bible passage on their Prayer Practice, John 15:5, from Eugene Peterson's Bible paraphrase, *The Message*:

> (Jesus said,) "I am the Vine, you are the branches. When you're joined with me and I with you, the relation intimate and organic, the harvest is sure to be abundant. Separated, you can't produce a thing."

Invite the group to respond to this passage and to the image of the vine and branches.

> What is the balance of human and divine power in this passage?

> How do the two support each other and not just conflict or compete?

After a few reflections about this, invite everyone into the closing prayer.

Closing Prayer

Have everyone stand and gather together. Pass out this week's memory gift—a piece of ivy. Invite the group members to hold their ivy, shut their eyes, and listen as you slowly read the following:

"You are a branch, and you are strongly attached to a vine. Feel your feet planted on that vine. Feel yourself able to draw nourishment and strength from that vine. Feel how it stabilizes you, how it connects you to the ground. And now, feel yourself growing from that stem, sprouting new leaves, reaching out into the world with new branches. You are connected to Jesus, rooted in his power, and able to grow in your own. Go in peace."

Memory Gift

The Memory Gift for this week is a sprig of ivy for each person.

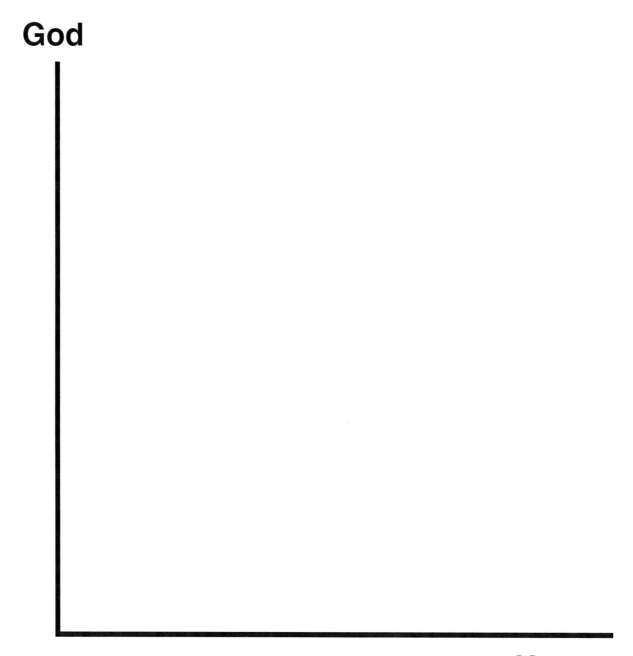

God

Human

"I have a friend who will pray for a parking place. Do you think God is involved in that level of detail in your life?"

"I don't think there are any accidents in life. Don't you agree?"

"I think my house might be haunted. Do you think a minister or a priest might be able to help us out?"

(Permission is granted to photocopy this page for use with *Talking Faith*.)

"I have a friend who's sick. I want to help him out, and I've been thinking about praying for him. But I'm not sure what to pray for. I don't want to set myself up for disappointment. What do you recommend?"

"Why do Christians always end their prayers by saying, 'In Jesus' name'? Do they really think that his name has some kind of special power?"

(Permission is granted to photocopy this page for use with *Talking Faith*.)

Session 3 Prayer Practice

(Jesus said,) "I am the Vine, you are the branches. When you're joined with me and I with you, the relation intimate and organic, the harvest is sure to be abundant. Separated, you can't produce a thing."

(John 15:5, *The Message*)

This week, as you pray, imagine yourself to be a branch, attached to a vine. When you need to, imagine yourself drawing strength and nourishment from the Vine. When you need to, imagine yourself reaching out into the world with leaves of your own. Let these images become your prayer. Use your journal to record any reflections or insights you might have.

Session 3 Prayer Practice

(Jesus said,) "I am the Vine, you are the branches. When you're joined with me and I with you, the relation intimate and organic, the harvest is sure to be abundant. Separated, you can't produce a thing."

(John 15:5, *The Message*)

This week, as you pray, imagine yourself to be a branch, attached to a vine. When you need to, imagine yourself drawing strength and nourishment from the Vine. When you need to, imagine yourself reaching out into the world with leaves of your own. Let these images become your prayer. Use your journal to record any reflections or insights you might have.

"Why Do Bad Things Happen?"

Song—5 minutes

Meal—30 minutes

Large Talk—25 minutes

    Jesus stations—15 minutes

    Discussion in pairs—10 minutes

Theme Talk—30 minutes

    Insights from Large Talk—5 minutes

    Responses to suffering in our lives—10 minutes

    Make a connection with scripture—10 minutes

    Make a connection with God's power—5 minutes

Real World—30 minutes

Prayer Practice—10 minutes

Closing Prayer—15 minutes

Memory Gift—Small candles

"Why Do Bad Things Happen?"

OBJECTIVES

To examine the many ways we might make sense of suffering and to experience Jesus' response to us in suffering.

MATERIALS

- Newsprint flipchart
- Easel
- Masking tape
- Newsprint from session 3 with chart of God's power and human power
- Colored dot stickers in red and green.
- All materials needed for the Jesus stations (see pages 44–57 at the end of the session)
- Prayer Practice sheets
- Memory Gifts: Small votive candles—enough for each member of the group to have one
- Glue sticks
- A few extra notebooks
- Pictures of Images of God that the participants drew in session 3

PREPARATION

- Write song lyrics on newsprint.
- Purchase small candles for Memory Gift.
- Set up the newsprint and easel, and chairs if you need to.
- Set up Jesus stations ahead of time. Ideally, set them up in the same space as the discussion part of the session. See pages 44–57 for Jesus station materials and instructions.
- Write Large Talk discussion question on newsprint.

Session Outline

Song

Suggestions for this week's song include: "Be Thou My Vision," "Softly and Tenderly," "What Wondrous Love Is This," or "Beauty for Ashes."

Meal

Large Talk

As the meal winds to a close, invite everyone to walk around the room, surveying the "Jesus Stations" you have set up with scripture and an object or image. Ask the group members to bring their prayer journals along, and have some paper on hand to offer those who have forgotten their journals. Ask each participant to survey all the stations and then to choose one or two images to which he or she is particularly drawn. Invite group members to sit near those stations for a while and record in their journals their thoughts about what the images mean to them and why they find those particular images engaging.

After about five to seven minutes, or when people seem ready, invite the participants to find partners. Post the newsprint sheet with the Large Talk question:

> How might this image be a response to suffering?

Make sure everyone understands the question and then let people talk for another five to seven minutes. Give a warning two minutes before closing to be sure both partners have had a chance to share.

Theme Talk

Insights from Large Talk

As you draw the group back together, ask if any of the pairs had a particular insight from their meditation and conversation that they would like to share with the group. At this point, the participants could share their thoughts largely without response from the leader, but listen for any insights about God's response to suffering that might be useful later in the discussion.

Responses to suffering in our lives

After some brief sharing, remind the group that as Christians, one of our central tasks is to make connections between all of what we have come to know about God through scripture, tradition, reason, and experience (remember session 2). This is not always easy to do—sometimes our experiences are perplexing. Suffering can be especially confounding as we wonder how a good and powerful God could create a world in which innocent people suffer terribly. Let the group consider this question for a moment before springing to answer it.

Explain to the group that we will begin to consider the question of God's response to suffering by grounding the discussion in our own experience. Ask the participants to recall a painful or difficult experience in their own lives. Use a fresh sheet of newsprint and write "Responses to Suffering" at the top. Ask the participants to list some ways in which they, or other people, responded to the painful experiences they recalled. What are some things people said to them? What are some things people did for them? What did they say and do for themselves? Some people might talk about various theological explanations that people offered, but the conversation should not go there too quickly. Encourage people to be very specific and experiential. Did people accompany them to doctor's appointments? Did they find others with similar experiences? Also, be sure to elicit stories of responses that were *not* helpful.

After you have compiled as extensive a list as possible, pass out colored sticky dots to everyone. If you have these, make a key at the bottom of your newsprint. RED=UNHELPFUL, GREEN=HELPFUL. Tell the participants that they should stick a green dot by any responses they felt were helpful—and they can even stick more than one dot by a response that they found extremely helpful. Then they can use red dots to vote for which responses were the least helpful. When the voting is done, encourage the group members to comment on any trends or points of consensus they see.

Make a connection with scripture

Now ask group members to consider the stories and images from the Bible that they interacted with earlier. Is there a connection between the images they were attracted to in scripture and the responses to suffering they have found helpful in their lives?

Posing this question, you are asking the participants to make a big leap. Some will be able to do it more easily than others. If your group is well able to handle this question, you may be able to let this conversation unfold without much direction from a leader. If this question stumps your group, be sure to have some possible connections ready to get their thoughts flowing. For example, you might make a connection between the healing of the blind man and those who found comfort in physical touch. Or, those who found it important to have their suffering acknowledged and named might make a connection with the bleeding woman. If no one mentions the crucifixion, you may want to raise the question yourself—can we make any connection between the cross and our own experience of suffering? What does it tell us about who God is?

Make a connection with God's power

If your group has exhausted its attention or time on the previous question, move on now to Real World. If you have the energy for a little more conversation, hand out the images of God that everyone drew the week before. Remind the group that we discussed the image of power implied in each drawing. Ask each person to consider which response to suffering, either on the newsprint list or in scripture, best fits the kind of divine power that is expressed in her or his picture. Invite anyone who would like to share his or her thoughts to do so.

Real World

If the group members need a break at this point, invite them to stand up and stretch for a moment. It might help to rearrange the chairs— you might want to make a circle of chairs with two in the middle to facilitate playing "Fishbowl." When the group is ready, explain that this week, there is only one question, and you are going to ask it. Sit on one of the chairs in the center of the circle. Explain that after you ask the question, you are going to invite anyone who would like to respond to come and sit in the seat next to you. The group's goal will be to try to keep the conversation flowing. At any time in the conversation, a member of the group can stand and tap one of the people in the "Fishbowl" on the shoulder and sit down in her or his place, substituting for either the person asking the question or the person responding. You may want to increase the "game" feeling by saying that the goal will be to keep the conversation going for five minutes, or ten minutes, and/or to include each member of the group.

When the group understands the rules of the game, begin with your question:

> I'm going through a very rough time right now, and I'm really having a hard time figuring out where God is in all of this. You go to church, right? Can you help me?

After the time is up, open the discussion. Did people use some of the "helpful" responses from your list? Which ones? What felt easy to say? What felt hard to say? What could you imagine saying to a friend? What could you imagine saying to someone you did not know well?

Prayer Practice

Pass out the Prayer Practice sheets and the glue sticks so that people can glue the sheets into their notebooks. Also, give each person a candle.

Explain that for this week we are going to experience intercessory prayer in a new way. When there is a person, a situation, a country that we want to lift up to God, we are going to imagine that we are holding them in the light. Tell people that they can light their candles before they pray and use that light to focus on during prayer time. Suggest that they hold their prayer partners in the light each day when they pray.

Closing Prayer

For the closing prayer, invite everyone to light his or her new Memory Gift candles. Then read John 8:12:

Again Jesus spoke to them, saying, "I am the light of the world. Whoever follows me will never walk in darkness but will have the light of life."

Invite people to imagine the light Jesus is talking about. That light is always burning. Encourage people to speak aloud the names of people or places in the world that need the light of Christ.

Memory Gift

Each person should receive a small candle to be lit during Prayer Practice time this week.

Set Up for Jesus Station Exercise

Objective

To create an exercise in which people interact with the Bible and symbolic objects in order to deepen their relationship with Jesus Christ and to see how all of his life might be viewed as a response to suffering.

Materials

- Jesus Station Bible quotations printed and cut out. See pages 45–57. (Each quote should be on its own slip of paper.)
- An object for each Bible quotation. The suggested objects are:

  Stuffed animal or toy lamb. John 1:29
  Gauze or a bandage. Mark 5:25–34
  A small lump of modeling clay. John 9:1–7
  A candle (and matches). John 8:12
  A vine or a leafy plant. John 15:1–8
  A shiny paper star. Revelation 22:16
  A shepherd—a shepherd from a crèche would be perfect. John 10:11–18
  A toy hen or a picture of a hen. Luke 13:34
  A Bible opened to Isaiah. Luke 4:16–21
  A loaf of bread. John 6:35
  Crèche figures of Mary, Joseph, Jesus, and the angel. Matthew 1:18–25
  A bowl of water and a towel. John 13:3–17
  A cross. Matthew 27:27–37

(If you cannot collect all the suggested items for the exercise, you may simply make do with images we have provided on the Jesus Station Bible Passages sheets.)

- Tables and chairs
- Something to put the objects on top of—cloth, sheets of construction paper, napkins
- Audiocassette or CD player and some recordings of quiet music

Preparation

Put up tables around the room. If your tables are large, you can put two to four stations at one table. Make sure each table has enough room for each Jesus station. The stations need to be distinct so that people have the space they need to interact with the Bible passage and the objects on the table. At each station, place a chair. (Some tables may have more than one chair.)

Place some sort of cloth or piece of paper at each station and then put the Bible passage and its corresponding object at the station. Make the stations as aesthetically pleasing as you can.

Cue the music so that you are ready to go when you do the exercise. Follow the instructions in the session Large Talk section.

John 1:29

The next day [John the Baptist] saw Jesus coming toward him and declared, "Here is the **Lamb of God** who takes away the sin of the world!"

Mark 5:25–34

Now there was a woman who had been suffering from hemorrhages for twelve years. She had endured much under many physicians, and had spent all that she had; and she was no better, but rather grew worse. She had heard about Jesus, and came up behind him in the crowd and touched his cloak, for she said, "If I but touch his clothes, I will be made well." Immediately her hemorrhage stopped; and she felt in her body that she was **healed** of her disease. Immediately aware that power had gone forth from him, Jesus turned about in the crowd and said, "Who touched my clothes?" And his disciples said to him, "You see the crowd pressing in on you; how can you say, 'Who touched me?'" He looked all around to see who had done it. But the woman, knowing what had happened to her, came in fear and trembling, fell down before him, and told him the whole truth. He said to her, "Daughter, your faith has made you well; go in peace, and be healed of your disease."

John 9:1–7

As he walked along, he saw a man blind from birth. His disciples asked him, "Rabbi, who sinned, this man or his parents, that he was born blind?" Jesus answered, "Neither this man nor his parents sinned; he was born blind so that God's works might be revealed in him. We must work the works of him who sent me while it is day; night is coming when no one can work. As long as I am in the world, I am the light of the world." When he had said this, he spat on the ground and made **mud** with the saliva and spread the mud on the man's eyes, saying to him, "Go, wash in the pool of Siloam" (which means Sent). Then he went and washed and came back able to see.

John 8:12

Again Jesus spoke to them, saying, "I am the **light** of the world. Whoever follows me will never walk in darkness but will have the light of life."

John 15:1–8

"I am the true **vine**, and my Father is the vinegrower. He removes every branch in me that bears no fruit. Every branch that bears fruit he prunes to make it bear more fruit. You have already been cleansed by the word that I have spoken to you. Abide in me as I abide in you. Just as the branch cannot bear fruit by itself unless it abides in the vine, neither can you unless you abide in me. I am the vine, you are the branches. Those who abide in me and I in them bear much fruit, because apart from me you can do nothing. Whoever does not abide in me is thrown away like a branch and withers; such branches are gathered, thrown into the fire, and burned. If you abide in me, and my words abide in you, ask for whatever you wish, and it will be done for you. My Father is glorified by this, that you bear much fruit and become my disciples."

(Permission is granted to photocopy this page for use with *Talking Faith.*)

Revelation 22:16

[Jesus said,] "I am the **root** and the descendant of David, the bright **morning star.**"

John 10:11–18

"I am the **good shepherd**. The good shepherd lays down his life for the sheep. The hired hand, who is not the shepherd and does not own the sheep, sees the wolf coming and leaves the sheep and runs away—and the wolf snatches them and scatters them. The hired hand runs away because a hired hand does not care for the sheep. I am the good shepherd. I know my own and my own know me, just as the Father knows me and I know the Father. And I lay down my life for the sheep. I have other sheep that do not belong to this fold. I must bring them also, and they will listen to my voice. So there will be one flock, one shepherd. For this reason the Father loves me, because I lay down my life in order to take it up again. No one takes it from me, but I lay it down of my own accord. I have power to lay it down, and I have power to take it up again. I have received this command from my Father."

Luke 13:34

"Jerusalem, Jerusalem, the city that kills the prophets and stones those who are sent to it! How often have I desired to gather your children together as a **hen** gathers her brood under her wings, and you were not willing!"

(Permission is granted to photocopy this page for use with *Talking Faith*.)

Luke 4:16–21

When [Jesus] came to Nazareth, where he had been brought up, he went to the synagogue on the sabbath day, as was his custom. He stood up to read, and the **scroll** of the prophet Isaiah was given to him. He unrolled the scroll and found the place where it was written:

"The Spirit of the Lord is upon me,
    because he has anointed me
        to bring good news to the poor.
He has sent me to proclaim release to the captives
    and recovery of sight to the blind,
        to let the oppressed go free,
to proclaim the year of the Lord's favor."

And he rolled up the scroll, gave it back to the attendant, and sat down. The eyes of all in the synagogue were fixed on him. Then he began to say to them, "Today this scripture has been fulfilled in your hearing."

(Permission is granted to photocopy this page for use with *Talking Faith*.)

John 6:35

Jesus said to them, "I am the **bread** of life. Whoever comes to me will never be hungry, and whoever believes in me will never be thirsty."

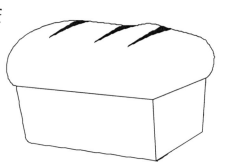

(Permission is granted to photocopy this page for use with Talking Faith.)

Matthew 1:18–25

Now the birth of **Jesus** the Messiah took place in this way. When his mother **Mary** had been engaged to **Joseph,** but before they lived together, she was found to be with child from the Holy Spirit. Her husband Joseph, being a righteous man and unwilling to expose her to public disgrace, planned to dismiss her quietly. But just when he had resolved to do this, an **angel** of the Lord appeared to him in a dream and said, "Joseph, son of David, do not be afraid to take Mary as your wife, for the child conceived in her is from the Holy Spirit. She will bear a son, and you are to name him Jesus, for he will save his people from their sins." All this took place to fulfill what had been spoken by the Lord through the prophet:

"Look, the virgin shall conceive
and bear a son,
and they shall name him Emmanuel,"

which means, "God is with us." When Joseph awoke from sleep, he did as the angel of the Lord commanded him; he took her as his wife, but had no marital relations with her until she had borne a son; and he named him Jesus.

(Permission is granted to photocopy this page for use with *Talking Faith.*)

John 13:3–17

Jesus, knowing that the Father had given all things into his hands, and that he had come from God and was going to God, got up from the table, took off his outer robe, and tied a **towel** around himself. Then he poured **water into a basin** and began to wash the disciples' feet and to wipe them with the towel that was tied around him. He came to Simon Peter, who said to him, "Lord, are you going to wash my feet?" Jesus answered, "You do not know now what I am doing, but later you will understand." Peter said to him, "You will never wash my feet." Jesus answered, "Unless I wash you, you have no share with me." Simon Peter said to him, "Lord, not my feet only but also my hands and my head!" Jesus said to him, "One who has bathed does not need to wash, except for the feet, but is entirely clean. And you are clean, though not all of you." For he knew who was to betray him; for this reason he said, "Not all of you are clean."

After he had washed their feet, had put on his robe, and had returned to the table, he said to them, "Do you know what I have done to you? You call me Teacher and Lord— and you are right, for that is what I am. So if I, your Lord and Teacher, have washed your feet, you also ought to wash one another's feet. For I have set you an example, that you also should do as I have done to you. Very truly, I tell you, servants are not greater than their master, nor are messengers greater than the one who sent them. If you know these things, you are blessed if you do them."

(Permission is granted to photocopy this page for use with *Talking Faith*.)

Matthew 27:27–37

Then the soldiers of the governor took Jesus into the governor's headquarters, and they gathered the whole cohort around him. They stripped him and put a scarlet robe on him, and after twisting some thorns into a crown, they put it on his head. They put a reed in his right hand and knelt before him and mocked him, saying, "Hail, King of the Jews!" They spat on him, and took the reed and struck him on the head. After mocking him, they stripped him of the robe and put his own clothes on him. Then they led him away to crucify him.

As they went out, they came upon a man from Cyrene named Simon; they compelled this man to carry his **cross.** And when they came to a place called Golgotha (which means Place of a Skull), they offered him wine to drink, mixed with gall; but when he tasted it, he would not drink it. And when they had crucified him, they divided his clothes among themselves by casting lots; then they sat down there and kept watch over him. Over his head they put the charge against him, which read, "This is Jesus, the King of the Jews."

(Permission is granted to photocopy this page for use with *Talking Faith*.)

Prayer Practice

> ## Session 4 Prayer Practice
>
> During your daily prayer time, light your Memory Gift candle. Feel the heat it gives. Notice its brilliance. See how strong the flame is. Now, imagine the people, the places, and the situations in your life that are in need of that light. Take time to hold each one of them in the light of Christ.

> ## Session 4 Prayer Practice
>
> During your daily prayer time, light your Memory Gift candle. Feel the heat it gives. Notice its brilliance. See how strong the flame is. Now, imagine the people, the places, and the situations in your life that are in need of that light. Take time to hold each one of them in the light of Christ.

> ## Session 4 Prayer Practice
>
> During your daily prayer time, light your Memory Gift candle. Feel the heat it gives. Notice its brilliance. See how strong the flame is. Now, imagine the people, the places, and the situations in your life that are in need of that light. Take time to hold each one of them in the light of Christ.

(Permission is granted to photocopy this page for use with *Talking Faith*.)

"Who's to Say What's Right and Wrong?"

Song—5 minutes

Meal—30 minutes

Large Talk—What would Jesus drive?—10 minutes

Theme Talk—40 minutes

    What does it mean to be a disciple?—10 minutes

    It's hard to be a disciple—even in the Bible—10 minutes

    Let's vote on culture—20 minutes

Real World—30 minutes

Prayer Practice—5 minutes

Closing Prayer—10 minutes

Memory Gift—Invitation cards

"Who's to Say What's Right and Wrong?"

OBJECTIVE

To help the participants consider how we can engage with our culture in a way that witnesses to the way of Jesus.

MATERIALS

- Newsprint
- Masking tape
- Easel
- Big black marker
- A CD or cassette player
- Music. You have a couple of different options this week. You could bring in some popular, secular music that you feel has spiritual significance, or a recording of contemporary Christian music that has a pop sound. Or, if you have access to the sound track to *Sister Act*, you could bring that in!
- Bibles for everyone—different translations or versions are fine
- Red, yellow, and green paper, preferably card stock
- Glue sticks or tape
- Invitation cards. Find a pack of inexpensive party invitations at the grocery or drug store. They can simply say "You're Invited" or they can have spaces in which you fill in information. While it is better if they do not say "To a Birthday Party," they can be playful!
- Basket or cup
- Index cards or slips of paper

PREPARATION

- Write the song lyrics on newsprint, and hang them in a prominent place in your meeting room.
- Set up the newsprint and easel, and chairs if you need to.
- Make sure Bibles are on hand. Mark one of the following passages in three of them: Romans 12:2; 1 Corinthians 9:19–23; Matthew 26:26–29.
- Make one red, one yellow and one green voting card for each participant. Copy the attached form onto colored card stock and cut. Put a plus sign (+) on the green card, a minus sign (-) on the red card, and a neutral sign (~) on the yellow card. If you do not have colored paper, you can do this on white paper, though it makes it harder to count votes.
- Prepare the questions for the Real World role plays. Copy the questions on pages 64–65. Cut the questions apart, fold them, and put them in a basket or cup.
- Copy this week's Prayer Practice, and cut out one for each person in the group.
- Get this week's Memory Gift ready—write "Jesus" on the front of each invitation envelope. Do not seal the envelopes.

Session Outline

Song

This week, try singing a popular song that can become a song of praise to God. Go with an oldie that most people will know! Suggestions include: "Have I Told You Lately that I Love You?" "How Sweet It Is (to Be Loved by You)." Or, try singing the version of "My Guy" from Sister Act ("My God").

Meal

As people eat, informally chat about how last week's Prayer Practice went, and how people are feeling about *Talking Faith* in general. Does anyone have any issues or concerns?

Large Talk

As a whole group, have some fun brainstorming about what Jesus would be like if he were to live among us today. Invite someone in the group to record the group's brainstorms on newsprint. Ask questions such as the following:

> WWJD—What Would Jesus Drive?
>
> What profession would he have?
>
> Who would he like to hang out with? Where would he live?
>
> Would he go to church? Would he go to your (our) church?

After you brainstorm, take a minute to reflect on what you just said:

> What do your comments say about who we think Jesus is?
>
> What do your comments say about our world?
>
> Would Jesus be at home among us?

Theme Talk

What does it mean to be a disciple?

Remind the group that the focus for this session is the question, "How are we supposed to live our lives?" For Christians, the conversation we just had is closely related to this question because Jesus invited his followers to follow him, to become his disciples, and to live as he did. Invite the group to begin by remembering the kind of life that Jesus lived, what he taught, and what he told his disciples to do.

Have the group members brainstorm a list, and write their responses on newsprint. If they are having trouble, or if you feel there are big gaps in their responses, you can always ask prompting questions:

> We have talked about what Jesus said, but what about what he did?
>
> Who did Jesus spend time with?
>
> What kinds of activities were important to his ministry?

It's hard to be a disciple—even in the Bible

It is one thing to list these things, to talk about them. It is another thing entirely to try to live them out. Jesus' first followers struggled with lots of questions about how to live as his disciples in the world, and the conversation was a huge one in the early church as well.

Pass out the Bibles, and invite three people to read one of the following passages: Romans 12:2; 1 Corinthians 9:19–23; Matthew 26:26–29. After each reading, invite the group to consider the view of culture, the world outside the community of disciples, that is expressed in the passage. Evaluate each passage briefly, and then move to the next one. Then take some time to notice the contrasts between the passages. You might summarize it this way: in Romans, culture is negative, something to be warned against. In 1 Corinthians, culture is a tool for Paul—he'll "speak the language" as long as he can get his point across. In the Matthew story, Jesus is using the symbols of his culture, the elements of the Passover table, in a way that underscores their importance. Here, culture is positive.

Let's vote on culture

When you feel like the group members have a basic grasp of the distinction between a positive, negative, and neutral view of culture in the Bible, pass out the voting cards and explain that they are going to vote on various aspects of our current culture, whether the aspects should be regarded as positive, negative, or neutral tools by Jesus' modern-day disciples. Explain that the green card with the "+" sign means that something is positive, helpful, supportive to Jesus' disciples. The red card with the "-" sign means that something is negative, damaging to Jesus' disciples and to be resisted or defeated. The yellow card with the "~" means that something is neither positive nor negative, but it could be used by Jesus' disciples to do their work and spread Jesus' message. When everyone understands the idea, start throwing out some features of contemporary culture. Invite people to hold up a card in response, evaluating each feature as positive, negative, or neutral.

Pause for discussion whenever you need to, but do not get bogged down on any particular issue:

- Racism
- Music (Have some fun here—Opera? Rap? Heavy Metal?)
- Multiculturalism
- Commercialism
- Television
- The Internet
- Violence
- The growing acceptance of homosexuals
- Fast food
- Urban mobility
- The concentration of wealth
- Radio talk shows
- Tattoos
- Animal-rights activists

Add your own ideas of cultural features, and invite the group to do the same. When people start to run out of ideas, take some time to evaluate.

> Was there wide consensus among the group?
>
> Were there points of strong difference? Where? Why?
>
> What can we say in general about our orientation as people of faith to our contemporary culture?
>
> What aspects of our culture make it hardest to live as a disciple of Jesus? How should we as Christians respond?

Real World

When you have brought the previous conversation to a close, you might want to take a quick moment to stretch and relax before inviting the group into a conversation in which we apply the kind of discernment we have been doing to some conversations they might have in the real world. This week, you can choose which technique you feel would work best to get your group talking—responding as a panel, role plays, fish bowl, or some other method. (For example, you could invite people to pick a question and then pick someone in the group to answer it. Then, that person gets to pick the next question.)

This is also a good week to invite your group to help make up some of the questions—be sure to have extra index cards or slips of paper available. You may find that questions just bubble up, and people throw them out to the group. If that happens, go with it! Give yourself plenty of time for this exercise this week.

Prayer Practice

Pass out the instructions for the coming week, and invite people to glue or tape them into their journals. Then, hand out the invitation cards. Explain that this week we are going to experiment with inviting Jesus to be with us in every part of our non-church lives. Suggest that they try using the card to reinforce their Prayer Practice—putting it on the dashboard of their car, sticking it in their purse or bag, leaving it out on the kitchen counter. When they see it, have them simply say, "Jesus, I invite you here with me." Ask for any questions.

Closing Prayer

Invite the group to gather together and invite them to a few moments of quiet. Explain that when that time is over, each person is invited to pray aloud or silently, "Jesus, I invite you to…" whatever they wish. Perhaps there is something stressful coming up in their week, or an ongoing situation in their lives they feel like they need help with. Conclude with a prayer inviting Jesus to be with the group as a whole this week and to build each of us up as his disciples.

Memory Gift

This week the Jesus invitation cards are the Memory Gifts. Instructions on how to make them are under the "Preparation" section above.

"I go to churches and all they ever have is organ music. Who listens to organ music? When are churches going to realize that nobody listens to that any more?"

"I'm looking for a church to go to. I went to this one church and the minister preached on the war in Iraq. I don't think that a minister should put out his opinion on that from the pulpit. What do you think?"

"What's your church's stand on abortion?"

"Are you in favor of prayer in schools?"

"I like Jesus, but I really can't stand a lot of the Christians I've met. They lie and cheat and abuse people just as bad as anyone else does. What good is a church when the people inside it aren't living holy lives?"

"I don't think you have to believe in God to be a good person. Do you?"

"Do you really think churches should be tax-exempt?"

"I'm always disgusted when I see political candidates making appearances at churches. That just doesn't seem right to me. I mean, churches can take stands on issues, but not on candidates or political parties. Don't you agree?"

(Permission is granted to photocopy this page for use with *Talking Faith*.)

Prayer Practice

Session 5 Prayer Practice

You are invited to imagine Christ being present in particular situations you find yourself in this week. For example, as you are standing next to someone on the street corner, sitting next to someone in a hospital bed, eating breakfast with your family, arguing with a coworker, invite Christ to be with you in that moment. Imagine him there with you. In your prayer journals, you are invited to note the places you were when you imagined Jesus and to describe how the prayer affected you.

Session 5 Prayer Practice

You are invited to imagine Christ being present in particular situations you find yourself in this week. For example, as you are standing next to someone on the street corner, sitting next to someone in a hospital bed, eating breakfast with your family, arguing with a coworker, invite Christ to be with you in that moment. Imagine him there with you. In your prayer journals, you are invited to note the places you were when you imagined Jesus and to describe how the prayer affected you.

Session 5 Prayer Practice

You are invited to imagine Christ being present in particular situations you find yourself in this week. For example, as you are standing next to someone on the street corner, sitting next to someone in a hospital bed, eating breakfast with your family, arguing with a coworker, invite Christ to be with you in that moment. Imagine him there with you. In your prayer journals, you are invited to note the places you were when you imagined Jesus and to describe how the prayer affected you.

"Who's Invited?"

Special This Week—Take group photo—5 minutes

Song—5 minutes

Meal—30 minutes

Large Talk—20 minutes

    Taboo game—10 minutes

    "Why do you go to church?"—10 minutes

Theme Talk—30 minutes

    God's community: The great banquet—20 minutes

    What can and can't I bring to church?—10 minutes

Real World—30 minutes

Prayer Practice—10 minutes

Closing Prayer—10 minutes

Memory Gift—Laminated prayer cards

"Who's Invited?"

OBJECTIVE

For the participants to consider who is invited into their churches and into relationship with Jesus.

MATERIALS

- Newsprint flipchart
- Easel
- Masking tape
- Bell
- Table tents—Paper folded over to stand up like a tent
- Markers
- Communion elements—Wine or juice in a cup or chalice, bread
- Large candle and matches
- Self-laminating paper for laminated prayer cards
- Prayer Practice 6 sheets (copy and cut out page 74 for prayer journals)
- Glue sticks
- Camera—digital or film (You will need to take a picture of your group at this meeting so that you have time to develop your film to make the Memory Gift for the last gathering, session 8.)
- Bibles for everyone

PREPARATION

- Write the song lyrics on newsprint.
- Set up the newsprint and easel, and chairs if you need to.
- Make credit-card-size laminated prayer cards. You can use the sample at the end of the session on page 73.
- Set up communion ahead of time. You will need to find a space other than your meeting space to do the "Who's invited" exercise and to celebrate communion. Ideally, this will be in the sanctuary of your church. Have the elements and the large candle on the altar in the sanctuary. (Or you can create an altar in your room.) Make sure that there is space enough for everyone in the group to gather in a circle around the elements.
- Make your personal table tents before the session so that you can use them as an illustration for the "What can and can't I bring to church?" exercise. Write one quality about yourself on each tent. Make eight or so. Try to use a mixture of serious and lighthearted qualities. (For example: mother, minister, singer, nail biter, seeker, beer drinker, skeptic, Web site designer, worrier.) Remember, your modeling of honesty and vulnerability in the group will make a big difference in how much people are willing to open up.
- Make table tents for the group. Have enough folded so that every member of your group can have at least eight. (All you do is cut a piece of card stock in half. Then fold that half in half down the long side of the card.)

Session Outline

Special This Week

Take a picture of your group this week. You can do it before the session begins or after communion. You will use this picture for the Memory Gift for session 8.

Song

Suggestions for this week's song include: "Jesus Is Here Right Now," "Open My Eyes, Lord," "Glory, Glory, Hallelujah," or "More Precious Than Silver."

Meal

Large Talk

Tell the participants that this week we are going to make Large Talk into a bit of a game. First, we must brainstorm a bit. Ask the group members what answers they usually give when someone asks, "Why do you go to church?" As people answer the question, write their words or phrases on newsprint. You do not need to write everything a person says, but write key words such as *community*, *people*, *quiet*. After everyone has had a chance to respond to the question and offer a few answers, explain that the group is now going to play the game Taboo™.

In the game Taboo™, certain words are taboo. In other words, they cannot be used. People have to find a way to talk about a given topic without those words. For example, if someone were to try to describe what an ice cream cone was like, the taboo words might be *ice cream*, *cone*, *cold*, *sweet*, *summer*, and *lick*. The person would have to come up with creative ways to describe the qualities of an ice cream cone. Similarly, in Large Talk today, the participants are going to describe to their partners why they go to church without using the words that are on the newsprint. Those words are taboo.

As usual, divide the group into pairs, making sure that people are not talking to the same folks they did last week. Have the pairs answer the question, "Why do you go to church?" without the taboo words. When each pair has answered the question, ask them to discuss whether they have ever invited someone to church and to describe what that felt like. Did they use any of the taboo words when they invited the friend to church?

Give the participants eight to ten minutes to Large Talk. Ring the bell softly to indicate that the time is up.

Theme Talk

One of the most frequently asked questions of churchgoers by nonchurchgoers is "Why do you go to church?"

It is a really good question. Some of us who go to church are so conditioned to go (that's what we do on Sunday morning) that it is hard to answer the question without using some "in-house" language.

To start off the conversation, find out from people whether it was hard to talk about why they go to church without using the taboo words. If so, why? Often, people answer that they go to church for the community, the church family, or the nice people, but that could be true for any number of community groups.

> What is underneath the word *community* when we are talking about church?
>
> How is God's community different from civic community?
>
> What is it like to invite people to church?
>
> Is there anyone you would hesitate to invite to church? Is there anyone you think might not be welcome?

God's community: The great banquet

If the conversation is rolling, go with it. When your group is ready, invite them to open their Bibles to the story of the great banquet, Luke 14:15–24. Ask for two volunteers and have one read the passage, have some silent reflection time (a minute or two), and then ask the second person to read the passage again.

Ask your group the following questions, giving ample time for everyone to answer them. Don't feel that you have to get to them all.

Have you ever been to "the great banquet"?

What keeps you from the table?

When you think of this worshiping community, who isn't at the table?

What can and can't I bring to church?

When you feel that the group has had enough time with the text from Luke (half an hour maximum), move into the interactive exercise. Explain that the group is now going to be making table tents with qualities about themselves, one quality per table tent. Show the group the table tents that you have made ahead of time so that people understand what they look like and what is expected of them.

Pass out the prefolded table tents and a marker to each person. Have some extra table tents in the center of the table in case some people have more qualities that they want to write out.

Real World

When the participants have finished making their tents, explain that this week's Real World offers them a chance to see how much of themselves they are able to bring to church. Usually, when they do Real World exercises, they are having "dialogues" with seekers outside the church. Today, they are going to have an internal dialogue with a seeker inside the church, themselves.

Explain that they are going to place the table tents around the sanctuary (or in your meeting room if you have set up a place for communion there). They are going to show symbolically which parts of themselves they bring willingly to church and which parts feel less welcome. If people feel that they can bring the quality they have written on the tent to church, they are to

place that tent on or close to the communion table. If the quality is one that they do not bring to church, they are to place it near the back of the sanctuary (or very far away from the communion area) or even out the door. Other in-between qualities can be placed somewhere in the middle of the room, depending on how welcome that quality is in church. After you are sure that the group members understand what is expected of them, have them quietly enter the space and place their tents. This exercise should have a sacred, special feel.

When people have finished placing their tents, invite them to walk around the whole space and notice where people have put their tents.

After people have had the chance to look at all the tents, turn off all the lights, light the candle(s) on the communion table, and invite people to come to the table.

Begin to tell the story of the Last Supper. Feel free to create your own communion service, use one from your prayer book, or tell the story of the Last Supper by memory. You may also choose to read the communion liturgy printed on page 72. Do what feels most comfortable and faithful to you. All we ask is that you have a time in the liturgy when you invite the participants to gather up all the tents that are scattered throughout the room, and set them up all around the table. This act will be a physical reminder that Jesus Christ is large enough, strong enough, and loving enough to accept every part of who we are.

This tent exercise followed by the celebration of communion can be very powerful. You may choose to spend a few minutes giving people the time to talk about what the experience was like.

What did they notice? How did it feel?

How is their relationship with Jesus different from their relationship with the church? What would it take for them to bring their whole selves to church?

Prayer Practice

When it is clear that people are ready, explain that the Prayer Practice for the week is Prayer in Public Spaces. Pass out the laminated prayer cards and the Prayer Practice sheets for the week. (Pass out glue sticks or tape so participants can affix the sheets in their journals.)

Explain that the participants are asked to pray in public spaces. This week there are low-, medium-, and high-risk Prayer Practice options.

Low risk: Silently pray the prayer on the prayer card once a day when you are in a public place. The prayer card is the size of a credit card and should fit neatly in your wallet. For example, when you are getting your money out while standing in line at the grocery, pray the prayer.

Medium risk: Each day, when you are in a public place, notice people who you sense are in need of prayer. It could be the harried teller at the bank, the stressed-out mother with the out-of-control kids at the supermarket, or the sad-looking person sitting next to you on the subway. Pray for that person and, if you can, try to make eye contact with him or her.

High risk: Join with a friend (it could be your prayer partner or someone else) and pray aloud in a public place. You don't need to do it loudly. Just find a quiet spot on a bench in the mall, or on the wall outside the post office, and pray together. Pray in a way that is prayerful and spirit-filled for you.

For everybody, record what it felt like to pray this way in your prayer journal. Write down any questions or thoughts that you have. How was Jesus present to you this week?

Closing Prayer

Tell the group members that you are going to have a few minutes of silence, and after that quiet time, they are invited to lift up prayers of thanksgiving to God. As the leader, you can model prayers of thanksgiving by thanking God for all that God has given to your group during its meetings. Thank God for each participant and for those who make it possible for them to be there. Thank God for God's love and power in your church and in your community. Encourage everyone to say something aloud even it if is just one word.

Memory Gift

A laminated prayer card is this week's Memory Gift. Each participant is given a credit-card-size laminated prayer. You can copy and laminate the prayer at the end of this chapter, or you can write your own. Laminating them is necessary so that they can be taken out and put back in a wallet without tearing.

Communion Liturgy

We remember that on the night Jesus was betrayed, he invited his disciples to share a meal with him—people who were not perfect, people who made mistakes, people who were confused, people who often didn't get it when Jesus told them something, even people with the capacity to betray Jesus. But he invited them. He invited this imperfect, searching group of people to his table. Every part of them, even the parts that they weren't proud of or didn't understand, was invited to join him at the feast. Jesus invites us, today, we the disciples gathered here, to bring all of ourselves to him.

Let us gather up all of the tents, even those outside the door, and bring all those parts of ourselves to Jesus.

Have people collect up the tents and then set them up all around the table. You will now be sitting in a circle amidst all the tents. Continue with communion.

On that night, Jesus took the bread and after giving thanks, he broke it, and gave it to the disciples, saying:

"This is my body which is for you. Do this in remembrance of me."

In the same way, he took the cup saying:

"This is the new covenant in my blood. Do this, as often as you drink it, in remembrance of me."

Let us pray:

Lord God, having been called by Jesus to bring all of who we are to this table, we come to you. We are ready to receive you in this sacred meal. Send your Holy Spirit upon this bread and this cup so that they may be for us the feast of new life. Send your Holy Spirit upon us so that we may use all of who we are in the sharing of your good news. Send your Holy Spirit upon your church so that it might be a place where all are invited. This we pray in Jesus' name, Amen.

Share the elements together and then go right into the group closing prayer time.

Laminated Prayer Cards

Loving God, be with all the people gathered in this place. Help them to feel your presence and know you. Enable them to see beyond the tedium and routine of their daily lives and experience your love made known to us in Christ Jesus.

May my every word and action today show my love for you. In Jesus' name, I pray. Amen.

Loving God, be with all the people gathered in this place. Help them to feel your presence and know you. Enable them to see beyond the tedium and routine of their daily lives and experience your love made known to us in Christ Jesus.

May my every word and action today show my love for you. In Jesus' name, I pray. Amen.

Loving God, be with all the people gathered in this place. Help them to feel your presence and know you. Enable them to see beyond the tedium and routine of their daily lives and experience your love made known to us in Christ Jesus.

May my every word and action today show my love for you. In Jesus' name, I pray. Amen.

Prayer Practice

Session 6 Prayer Practice

Low Risk

Silently pray the prayer on the prayer card once a day when you are in a public place. The prayer card is the size of a credit card and should fit neatly in your wallet. For example, when you are getting your money out while standing in line at the grocery store, pray the prayer.

Medium Risk

Each day, when you are in a public place, notice people who you sense are in need for prayer. It could be the harried teller at the bank, the stressed-out mother with the out-of-control kids at the supermarket, or the sad-looking person sitting next to you on the subway. Pray for that person and, if you can, try to make eye contact with him or her.

High Risk

Join with a friend (it could be your prayer partner or someone else) and prayer aloud in a public place. You don't need to do it loudly. Just find a quiet spot on a bench in the mall, or on the wall outside the post office, and pray together. Pray in a way that is prayerful and spirit-filled for you.

For Everybody

Record what it felt like to pray this way in your prayer journal. Write down any questions or thoughts that you have. How was Jesus present to you this week?

(Permission is granted to photocopy this page for use with *Talking Faith*.)

"What about All the Other Religions?"

Song—5 minutes

Meal—30 minutes

Large Talk—Have you ever been converted?—10 minutes

Theme Talk—40 minutes

    Whom do you know? Who challenges you?—5 minutes

    How do we treat people of different faiths here and now?
       —15 minutes

    How does God treat people of different faiths in the end?
       —15 minutes

    How do the two columns relate? 5 minutes

Real World—30 minutes

Prayer Practice—10 minutes

Closing Prayer—10 minutes

Memory Gift—Lapel pins

"What about All the Other Religions?"

OBJECTIVE

To help the participants consider how they might best share their faith in a multireligious context.

MATERIALS

- Newsprint
- Masking tape
- Easel
- Big black marker
- Bibles for everyone—different translations or versions are fine.
- A "disguise" for the Real World activity—a pair of dark sunglasses, a Groucho Marx–style pair of glasses with attached nose and mustache, a trench coat and fedora or some other disguise of your own devising
- Glue sticks or tape
- Lapel pins
- Basket or cup

PREPARATION

- Write the song lyrics on newsprint, and hang them in a prominent place in your meeting room.
- Write this week's Large Talk questions on newsprint—but keep this sheet hidden until it is time for the exercise.
- Set up the newsprint and easel, and chairs if you need to.
- Be sure Bibles are on hand.
- Prepare the questions for the Real World role plays. Copy the questions on pages 80–81 and cut out each one. Fold them and put them in a basket or cup.
- Have your "disguise" on hand.
- Copy this week's Prayer Practice, and cut out one for each person in the group.
- Buy lapel pins, one for each member of the group. You can find resources online at http://www.automonline.com. Buy ones with a Christian symbol that fits your group.

Session Outline

Song

This week, try singing something that comes from another culture or tradition. Our suggestion is: "We Are Walking" ("Siyahamba/Caminando.") If you know a song that not everyone in the group would know, this is a good week to take a risk and teach it! Or, if there are strong singers in the group, invite them to help you teach a song.

Meal

Large Talk

Pair up the group members, and invite them to respond to one or more of the following questions, written on newsprint:

> Have you ever been converted? Religiously, politically, ideologically?

Give people time to talk, and then bring the whole group together and invite anyone to share some comments from her or his discussion. Be aware that this topic may be a source of great pain to some in your group. Acknowledge their feelings without attempting to defend or critique particular methods of evangelism, and encourage the group to do the same.

Theme Talk

Whom do you know? Who challenges you?

Write "What about all the other religions?" at the top of a piece of newsprint. Ask the group members if they know people who practice a different religion from them. Write down the faith traditions of their friends on newsprint. When people have said every one they can think of, keep probing. Has anyone ever met a Pagan? A Wiccan? Someone who is into New Age Spirituality? A Satanist?

When you have a long list, ask the group,

> Whom do you find it hardest to relate to or to understand?

> Has your faith ever been challenged by one of these people?

> Has your faith ever benefited from your relationship with one of these people?

Encourage people to tell specific stories, and encourage the group to listen without engaging in debate.

How do we treat people of different faiths here and now?

Draw a vertical line underneath the question on the newsprint, making two columns. Suggest that the question really has two parts:

> How do we treat people of different faiths here and now?

> What might their ultimate fate be, as determined by God?

Write "Us—Now" as the heading of one column, and "God—Future" as the heading of the other. Suggest that while these questions might be related to each other, they are not the same question.

Ask the group to brainstorm about what Jesus said about how we should treat people of different faiths here and now. If members have trouble thinking of a response, prompt them by asking how he taught his disciples to treat other people in general. Then ask if they can think of any situations in which Jesus interacted with someone of a different faith. How did he treat them? Remind them of the parable of the good Samaritan in which the person of a different faith was the one who did what was right.

Then, invite the group to open their Bibles to Mark 7:24–30, the story of the Syrophoenician woman. Invite someone to read the passage aloud, and then ask for reactions. Point out that the woman who challenges Jesus in this story is someone of a different faith tradition from his, and that initially he will not engage with her for that reason. But when she challenges him, he responds. Perhaps even Jesus learned something from someone of a different faith! This passage may help your group to move from a discussion of tolerance to a discussion of how we might be enriched by our conversations with people of different faiths.

How does God treat people of different faiths in the end?

There has been a great deal of debate on this point throughout Christian history, and there are three responses that have been prominent in Christian theology: An *exclusive* position, an *inclusive* position, and a *pluralist* position. These three categories will help the group members name their own beliefs, and you may want to simply write these three labels on the paper and explain them as follows:

> **Exclusive:** Only those who believe in Jesus will have eternal life.
>
> **Inclusive:** The truth in other religions will ultimately lead people to Jesus Christ in this life or the next.
>
> **Pluralist:** There are different kinds of truth, and different religions can be true in different ways. There is only one truth, and each religion only understands it in part.

Ask the group which of these categories best describes their position. Would they want to add other categories? Has their understanding of the categories changed over time?

How do the two columns relate?

Before moving to the next section, pose the question:

> Do your responses to the two different questions influence each other?

Real World

By this week, we think your group will be ready for some hard questions! Give them lots of affirmation before beginning—remind them of how much they have grown in talking comfortably about their faith, congratulate them for taking so many huge risks. Give specific examples of positive experiences you have had as a group in the context of these Real World exercises. Then tell them that this week the questions directly address the appropriateness of sharing our faith with people who are outside the church, and that they may at times touch on some of our real discomfort with that activity.

If one of the discussion formats from a previous session has gone particularly well in your group, you might suggest using it again in this session. Or, you might choose to do the following exercise if you think your group might respond well. This format is a way for us not only to laugh gently at ourselves but also to have the benefit of being "in disguise" while we take a risk in front of the group.

Faith under cover

Most of us live our lives as people of faith "under cover," that is, most of the people around us do not know or necessarily care about our commitment to our faith. Previous Real World exercises have focused on questions that non-church people will ask someone who they know is part of a faith community. The following comments are things we might hear, especially when the speaker does not know that the person he or she is speaking to is a person of faith.

To have a little fun with the exercise, provide an undercover disguise that can be passed around to whoever is responding to the question. This could be a pair of dark sunglasses, or a pair of Groucho Marx glasses with attached nose and mustache. If you have access to a trench coat and fedora (an undercover agent costume!), you could use those. Have some fun—it's disarming!—but don't get so elaborate that the costumes become distracting.

Have volunteers select a comment at random, and read it aloud to a volunteer in disguise. The challenge is to respond in a way that not only expresses the speaker's views but also reveals the speaker to be a person of faith. Is there a way in which the comment can be the beginning of a discussion, an opportunity for the responder to share something important about him- or herself? As the responder reveals who they really are, they take off their disguise!

After each person has had a chance to respond to a comment, open the discussion to the group.

Would anyone have responded differently?

What worked for them in the response?

After three or four turns, broaden the discussion.

What kinds of situations make us most want to share our faith?

What are the hardest situations for us to do so?

When it is time to bring the conversation to a close, distribute this week's Memory Gift, and briefly brainstorm with the group about how it might spark a conversation about faith with someone they know or with a stranger. What other ways are there to let people know that you would be open to having a conversation about faith?

Prayer Practice

Distribute the Prayer Practice instructions to the group, and invite them to tape or glue them into their journals. Have someone read the practice aloud, and make sure everyone understands it and has a moment to express feelings about it.

Be encouraging!

Closing Prayer

Have the group members gather together and pray for their ability to share their faith this week. You might say this prayer yourself, or you might invite the group members each to pray aloud for the person to their left, that they might be able to share their faith with honesty, integrity, and sensitivity. Invite the group members to put a hand on the shoulder of the person for whom they are praying.

Memory Gift

The Memory Gift for this week is a lapel pin for each participant. People may need some time to understand what the pin says and how they should wear it. Explain that this is a "conversation starter" that they can choose to wear around town. It is a little experiment to see if people notice and comment on their pin and to see how a conversation evolves when they do. Encourage folks to take a leap and wear the pin.

You might even pass them out and have the prayer partners "pin" each other and say a little prayer as they do so. (Those from a certain generation will enjoy the joke of "being pinned" again.) The pinning need not be too serious, but you should convey what adventurous people you have in your group to be wearing in public a symbol of their love of Jesus.

Real World Comments

"I'm a spiritual person, but I'm not religious!"

"I think all of the world's religions are really basically about the same thing. They all worship the same God. I think they all have something to teach."

"I think that at the heart of a lot of the world's problems is religion. Just look at all the wars that have been fought over religion! If we're ever going to stop killing each other, I think we're going to have to abandon religion, as John Lennon said in 'Imagine.'"

"I don't think it really matters what you believe—I think what's important is what you do. I think as long as you're a good person, you don't have anything to worry about."

"The Jehovah's Witnesses were at my door again yesterday. Those guys really annoy me! I wish they'd just keep their views to themselves. I mean, I don't go knocking on their door trying to convince them to think like I do!"

"Muslims are bloodthirsty and vicious. None of this conflict in the Middle East would be happening if they were all Christians!"

Prayer Practice

Session 7 Prayer Practice

This week, we invite you to take one of the following steps to reveal yourself to the world as a person who prays!

Low Risk

Invite your prayer partner to pray with you, either silently or aloud. Use your journal to record any feelings or reflections.

Medium Risk

Talk with someone who has a similar faith to you about his or her prayer life. Ask whether he or she prays, and what the experience is like for him or her. Share something about your prayer experiences. Use your journal to record any feelings or reflections.

High Risk

Talk with someone who has a different faith from you, or someone with no faith, about her or his experiences of prayer. Does he pray? What it is like for her? Share something about your prayer experiences. Use your journal to record any feelings or reflections.

For the Highly Adventurous Only!

Invite someone of a different faith, or someone with no faith, to pray with you. Use your journal to record any feelings or reflections.

"What Can I Hope For?"

Song—5 minutes

Meal—30 minutes

Large Talk—Have you ever had a glimpse of heaven?—10 minutes

Theme Talk—30 minutes

    Inviting ourselves and others to experience heaven—10 minutes

    The commissioning of the disciples—15 minutes

    You have enough—5 minutes

Memory Gift—Photo magnets

Closing Prayer—20 minutes

"What Can I Hope For?"

OBJECTIVES

To have the participants see that they are ready to begin sharing their faith *now* and to have them leave the course with a sense of hope made concrete in Jesus' continual presence with them.

MATERIALS

- Newsprint flipchart
- Easel
- Masking tape
- Bibles marked at Matthew 28:16
- Glue sticks
- Certificates
- Photo magnets of the group
- CD or audiocassette player
- CD or audiocassette of mellow music

PREPARATION

- Write the song lyrics on newsprint.
- Make a certificate for each group member. You can make your own or use the handout at the end of this session on page 88.
- Set up the newsprint and easel, and chairs if you need to.
- Make photo magnets of the group. There are two ways to do this:

    1. Buy clear plastic refrigerator magnet picture frames. You can find these at any large department store. Purchase one for each member of the group. Slide the group photo you took during session 6 into the frame and you are done.

    2. Laminate a group photo for each member. Then use adhesive magnetic tape and put the tape on the back of the laminated picture.

Session Outline

Song

Suggestions for this week's song include: "Leaning on the Everlasting Arms," "Lift Every Voice and Sing," or "Wellspring" ("River of Joy").

Meal

If you do have dinner, be sure you use some of your dinnertime to have the participants process the Prayer Practice of session 7. Everyone took some risks this past week in sharing her or his faith; be sure to affirm that!

Large Talk

Write on a piece of newsprint,

> "Have you ever had a glimpse of heaven?"

Before you begin the conversation, invite the group members to close their eyes for a moment, think of their responses, and remember the images and feelings the question calls to mind. After a minute, ask the group members to pair up. Invite everyone to respond to the question. Resist the temptation to define "heaven" in advance!

Theme Talk

Inviting ourselves and others to experience heaven

Bring the group back together, and invite everyone to share briefly his or her response to the Large Talk question.

After everyone has spoken, ask if anyone noticed some themes to what people shared.

> Were the experiences things that happened in the midst of daily life, or in the midst of extraordinary circumstances?
>
> Were they experiences of life here-and-now, or life after death?
>
> Is "heaven," as your group understands it, something that exists only after death, or does it break into the here-and-now?

Then ask,

> What would it feel like to invite someone into what you have just described?

Depending on the kinds of experiences people have shared, this question may stump some in the group. Don't give up—gently urge them to respond.

The commissioning of the disciples

When your group is ready, pass out the Bibles. Explain that since the start of the Christian church, faith sharing and the promise of eternal life have been linked. Today, we are going to look at the passage in the Bible when the disciples first learned that (1) There is definitely eternal life and (2) They have to share their relationship with Jesus with other people. Ask people to open their Bibles to Matthew 28:16–20. Ask for two volunteers and have one person read the passage, have some silent reflection time (a minute or two), and then ask the second person to read the passage again.

To get the conversation rolling, ask folks to put themselves in the position of the eleven disciples.

> You have just been told by the risen Christ that you are to go and make disciples of all the nations. You know the formula you are to use in baptism, but beyond that, you don't have a whole lot of instruction. What would you want to ask Jesus before he ascends into heaven?"

You can be both playful and serious with this as the mood of the group warrants. (Maybe the disciples would have liked a letter of reference from Jesus for their journey. Maybe they would have liked a talking-points sheet of possible questions they might be asked with the appropriate answers underneath. Maybe a corporate credit card or a company car would have helped. Even a manual or a book explaining just how to make disciples would have helped.) Feel free to list people's ideas on newsprint.

Follow-up questions could include,

Still being in the shoes (or sandals) of the disciples, what do you think gives you the authority to make disciples of all the nations?

Why do you think that some of your fellow disciples, or even you yourself, doubted when you first saw Jesus?

Why might you feel doubt even after the resurrection?

If it hasn't already come up in conversation, be sure to end with a question such as

What assurance or promise does Jesus give the disciples?

Spend some time talking about Jesus' statement "Remember, I am with you always, to the end of the age" (Mt. 28:20b).

You have enough

Note that while the disciples might have wanted to have a lot more instruction and direction from Jesus than they got (a letter of reference would have helped them open doors, a manual might have cleared up some of the problems that arose in Corinth), Jesus gave them something that could not be lost, stolen, or ruined by the elements—he gave them the assurance that life conquers death and he gave them his presence. He promised he would be with them. They didn't have to have all the answers or even a faith without doubt in order to be disciples. They had to know that Jesus, the conqueror of death, was with them and then start out on the journey into the world.

We are the same way. We might want more information, more books to read, more classes to take, but we have the same thing the first disciples had—the hope of eternal life with God and Jesus' presence with us until the end of the

age. We are ready. We have enough to get out there on the road.

What is more, the more we have conversations with other people about who Jesus is for us, the more real he is in our lives. Eternal life is not something that happens after we die, it is a relationship that starts now and grows as we grow in relationship to Jesus and all God's people. It all begins now.

Memory Gift

To introduce the last Memory Gift, you may want to say something like this:

You know, I often think that it would have been great if Jesus had lived in the age of the camera. Then we might have photos to go along with the stories in the Bible, visual pictures to show what it looked like when great moments in Jesus' life happened. But, there are a few images in the Bible I don't need to see photographically, because I already know what they looked like. One of those is the commissioning of the disciples on the last page of the gospel of Matthew. I already have a picture of what it looked like. Probably something like this.

Hold up one of the photo magnets that you have made and pass one out to everyone. Ask them to put the magnet on their refrigerator as a reminder of their call to share their faith. Tell the participants that when they get shy or scared about sharing their faith with others, they can look at this picture of the commissioning of the disciples and know that they are not the only ones out there sharing their faith, and that Jesus is with every one of them.

Continue on:

But for those of you who said that as disciples you would have liked a letter of recommendation or some kind of manual on how to do the job Jesus had given you, we have something for you as well—a certificate verifying that you are ready to share the good news of Jesus Christ.

Read each award certificate individually before handing them out. Encourage folks to clap for each person as you hand them out.

Closing Prayer

As this is the last meeting of the series, you may want to encourage each person to pray aloud in the group. This may help to emphasize that each person is equipped with what he or she needs to be a disciple of Jesus and share his or her faith.

However, should you choose to pray, be sure to give people enough time to celebrate the time they have spent together in the series and to say good-bye to this experience and welcome what is to come.

Consider ending the prayer time with a hymn or song.

You did it! Thanks be to God for all that you have accomplished together!

Achievement Certificate

_____

is awarded this certificate for completing

Talking Faith

You have a dynamic faith.
Now go out and share it!

_____

Printed in the United States
144479LV00003B/10/P